Introducing British Silver

Laura Bauld

First published in 2024 by Glasgow Museums Publishing.

ISBN 978-1-908638-44-1

Written by Laura Bauld
Edited by Fiona MacLeod
Designed by Jacqui Duffus
Photography by Enzo Di Cosmo, Jim Dunn, Maureen Kinnear, and Iona Shepherd
Reprographic scanning by Alan Broadfoot and Iona Shepherd
Images supplied by Glasgow Museums Photo Library

www.csgimages.org.uk
www.glasgowlife.org.uk/museums

Front cover image: Detail of 43.72
Back cover image: Detail of 43.16

Acknowledgements
With thanks to Rosemary Watt for her insights on the manuscript.

Printed in Scotland by MBM Print SCS Ltd, East Kilbride, Scotland
Cover printed on 350gsm Galerie Satin; text printed on 150gsm silk

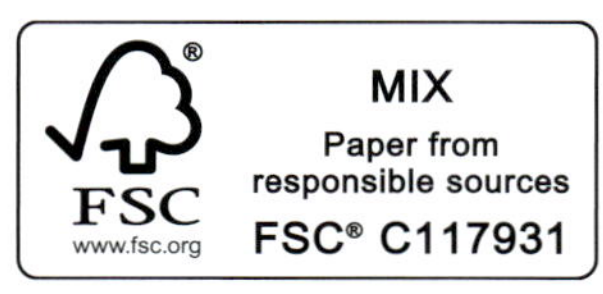

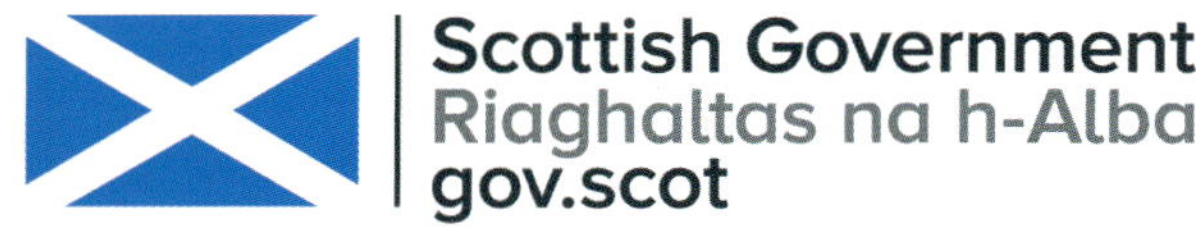

Contents

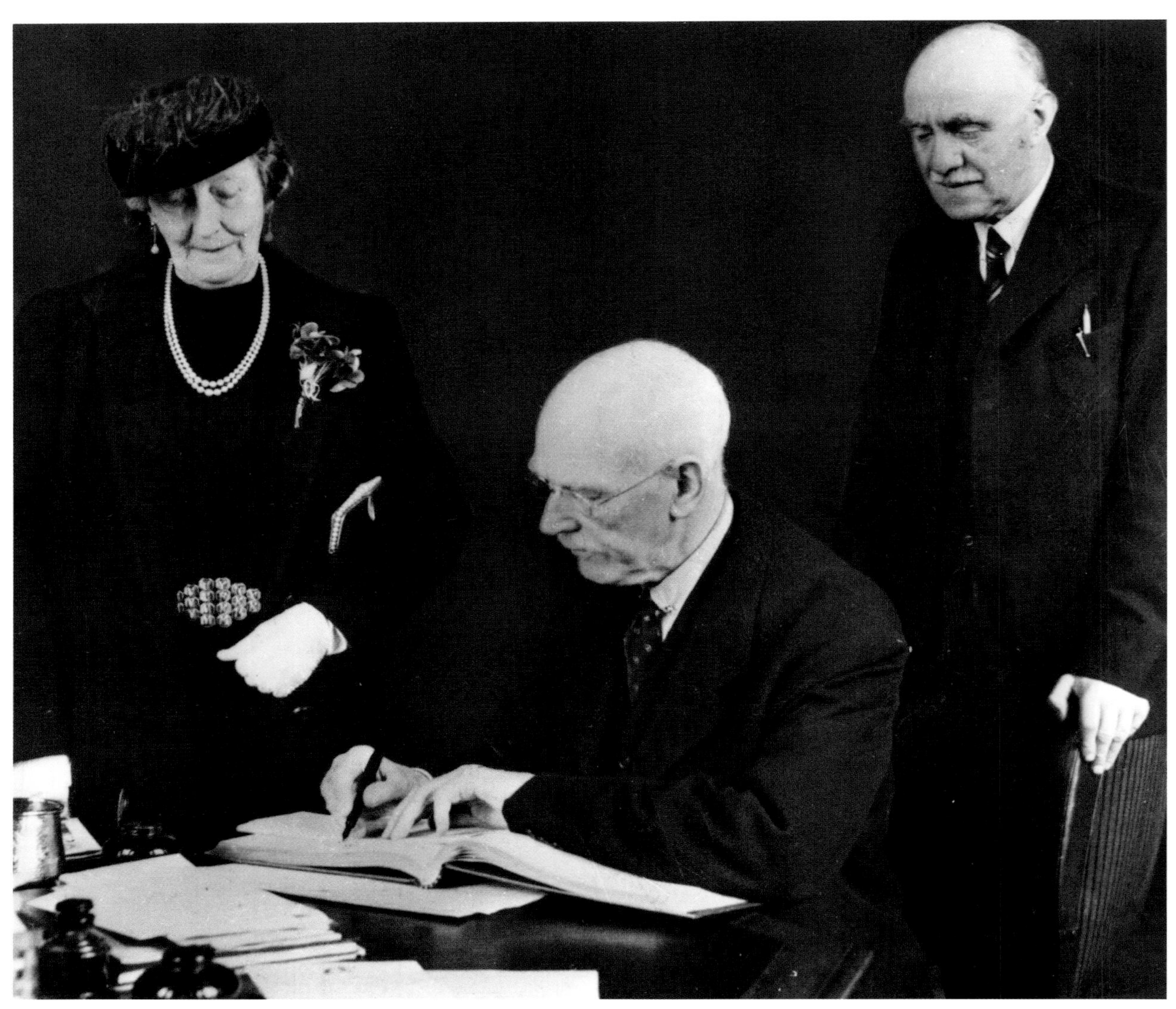

Sir William Burrell (seated), Constance, Lady Burrell and
Lord Provost James Welsh at the City Chambers, Glasgow,
1944, on the occasion of Sir William receiving the Freedom
of the City of Glasgow. Glasgow Museums Archive,
GMA.2013.1.1.470.

The Burrell Collection: The Gift of Sir William and Constance, Lady Burrell

The Burrell Collection comprises over 9,000 objects gifted to the city of Glasgow by Sir William Burrell (1861–1958) and his wife Constance, Lady Burrell (1875–1961). The main gift, of around 6,000 objects, was in 1944, but Burrell continued to add to it until his death, and the Collection has been further augmented with funds gifted by Burrell and administered by the Burrell Trustees.

Sir William made his fortune in shipping at a time when Glasgow was second city of the Empire. Collecting was a lifelong passion, and his treasures adorned his various homes: archive photographs show tapestries, sculpture, paintings and furniture in his house in Great Western Terrace, Glasgow. These, and also ceramics, stained glass, arms and armour and textiles, were displayed at Hutton Castle, his home in the Scottish Borders.

A sophisticated collector with a discerning eye, Burrell appreciated fine craftsmanship and meticulous attention to detail. From tapestries to sculpture, nineteenth-century French art to Chinese bronzes, medieval stained glass to Islamic carpets, the breadth and quality of his collection demonstrate his wide-ranging embrace of different cultures and art forms. Sir William also gave money for a new building to house his collection, and it is now displayed in a purpose-built museum in the centre of Pollok Country Park, on the south side of Glasgow. The park was gifted to the city in 1967 by Mrs Anne Maxwell Macdonald (1906–2011), and a competition, sponsored by the Royal Institute of British Architects, was held to design a suitable building within it to house the Collection. The winners of the competition, architects Barry Gasson, John Meunier and Brit Andresen, came up with a building which not only displays the Collection to advantage, but is also in harmony with the surrounding parkland. The building opened in 1983, but through the decades the Scottish weather took its toll and in 2016 the Category-A listed building closed for an ambitious programme of refurbishment, redisplay and reinterpretation.

This series is designed to introduce different parts of the Collection. Written by subject specialists, each book gives an insight into the Burrell's treasures. We, the Trustees of The Burrell Collection, are delighted to see the amount of new research that has been carried out on the objects in the collection, and hope that visitors will continue to enjoy Sir William and Constance, Lady Burrell's gift for many generations to come.

Professor Frances Fowle
Senior Trustee, Sir William Burrell's Trust

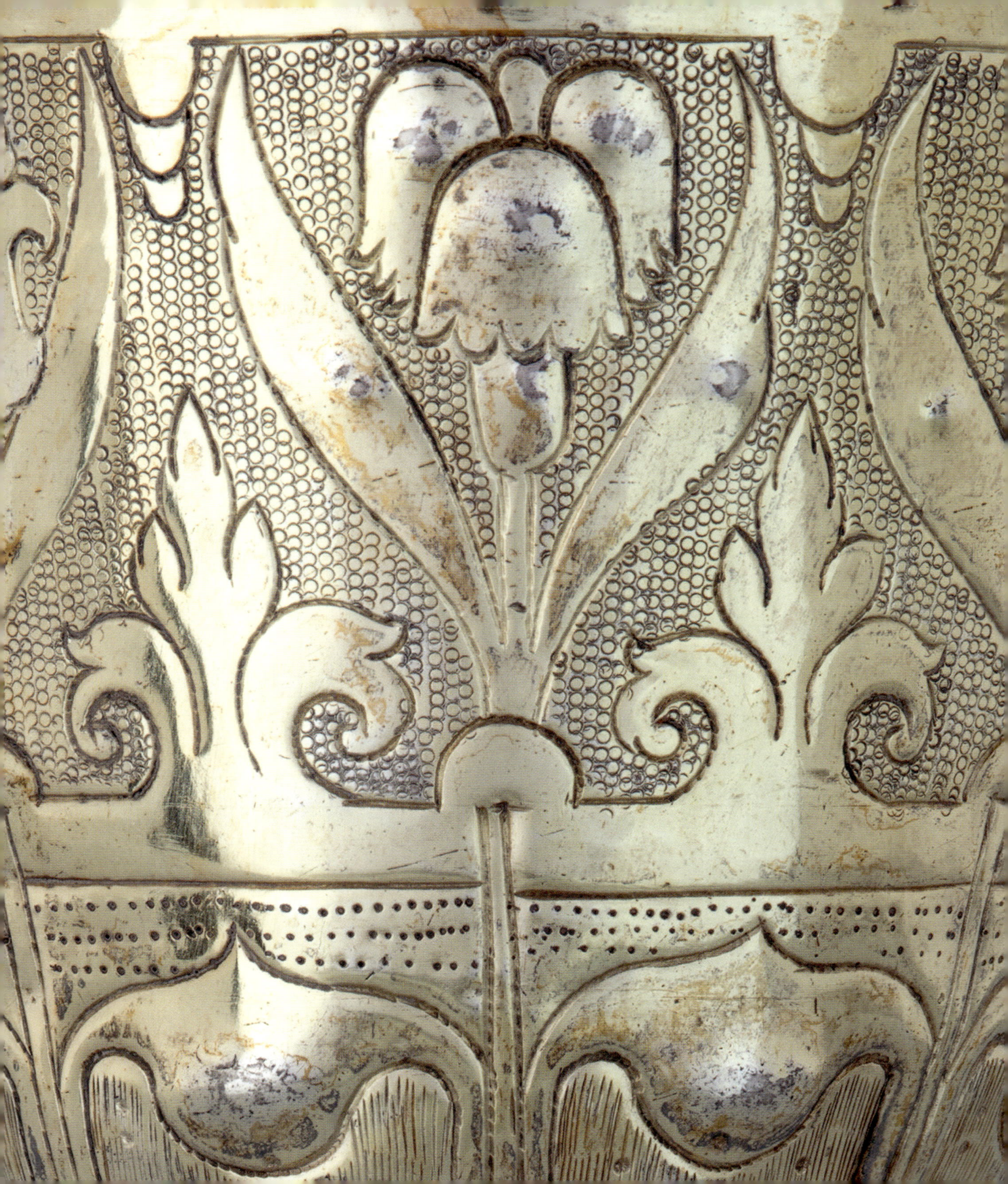

Collecting Silver

In 1947, Sir William Burrell wrote to the museum registrar of the Glasgow Corporation requesting to add a new silver object, a marrow spoon, to the art collection that he and his wife, Constance, had recently donated in 1944. In describing this spoon, Burrell wrote, 'It is late but plain. I feel that, speaking generally, the plain silver is the better'.

This tendency towards collecting 'plain' silver is reflected in the 240 British silver objects acquired by the Burrells. Representation of flamboyant rococo forms or refined neo-classism of the eighteenth century is sparse. Instead, the Burrells acquired a robust and expansive silver collection, demonstrating technical developments in manufacture and changing silver fashions from the fifteenth to late-eighteenth centuries, through fine examples of domestic, ecclesiastical, and ceremonial silver.

William Burrell purchased silver early in his collecting career. At the 1901 Glasgow International Exhibition, Burrell, then aged 39, was the biggest individual lender of art. He had an entire display case within the 'Art Objects' gallery allocated to his silver collection. From purchase records meticulously kept by Burrell from 1911, the silver collecting mostly took place from 1925–45, with additional pieces purchased after this time. Burrell acquired objects from leading London-based silver antique dealers including S.J. Phillips, Arthur & Co., and the Crichton Brothers. From the

1930s, many of his purchases were acquired from silver specialist David Black, of Black & Davidson, who were forerunners in silver trading at that time. The 1930s also saw Burrell loan his silver collection again; over 100 silver purchases made between 1937 and 1938 were lent directly to the Royal Scottish Museum in Edinburgh, raising Burrell's profile as an outstanding collector of silver.

Burrell's purchase records infrequently list the makers of the silver objects he bought but many pieces bear hallmarks, allowing identification of place of manufacture, date, and the names of notable silversmiths of the late-seventeenth and eighteenth centuries, including Huguenot metal-workers. Most of the collection can be attributed to London makers, but the Burrells also acquired silver from regional centres of silver manufacture, including Birmingham, Exeter, Newcastle, Norwich, Glasgow, and Edinburgh.

The Burrells set distinct parameters for their silver collecting with regards to date periods. They made numerous purchases of silver items ranging in date from the late-seventeenth to the late-eighteenth century but their tastes did not extend to items from the nineteenth century. In 1958, Constance Burrell was given the opportunity to purchase Victorian silver decorated with the Burrell coat of arms, a chance which she declined, stating 'It is late silver and too late for the collection'.

Opposite: Embossed and chased decoration on bowl of silver-gilt steeple cup purchased by Sir William Burrell in 1939 (detail; see also p.14–15).

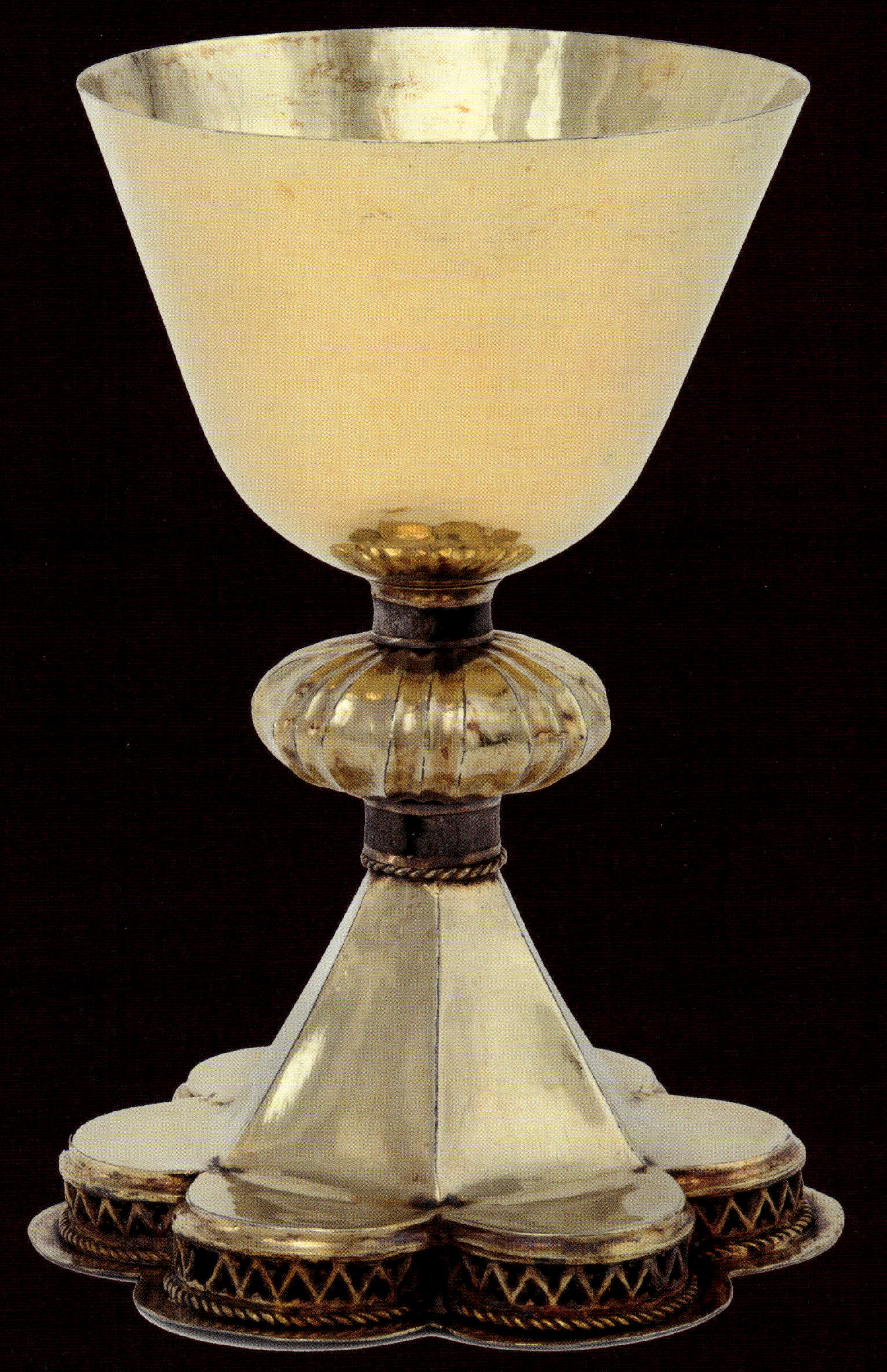

Ceremonial Silver

The Burrells' collection of silver demonstrates five centuries of British fascination in creating luxury silver objects for both religious and secular purposes. Objects fashioned from silver were also financial investments; the silver could be melted down when required and converted to cash. Silver had been used for coinage in Britain since ancient times by the Romans and Celts. From 1300 AD, silver coins were required to have 92.5% silver; it was referred to as the 'sterling' standard after the widely circulated silver 'sterling' penny. As silver could be converted into coin, the metal was valued in weight with essential systems of metal testing, known as assay, and marking created to enforce and maintain standards and protect currency.

Silver in its raw form is too soft to be worked into plate. The precious metal is alloyed, a process where the silver is mixed with metals like copper to strengthen it. Craftspeople who work with silver are known as silversmiths, or goldsmiths; historically they could work with both silver and gold, or one exclusively. The silversmith used different methods to create silver objects. The metal could be worked cold, the silversmith raising and forming the object from a flat sheet (ingot) of silver with the aid of rounded hammers, anvils, punches, tongs, and chisels. Silver can also be melted and formed into shapes with moulds in a process known as casting. Traditional silversmithing techniques are still used today to create silver objects.

Burrell's deep interest in Gothic and Medieval art led him to collect fifteenth- and sixteenth-century silver. The sixteenth century saw increased reserves of silver from European and South American mines entering circulation. The English crown also amassed silver from the removal of sacred silver objects from monasteries during the English Reformation. The ecclesiastical silver collected by the Burrells charts the changing styles of religious silver objects influenced by this turbulent time of religious reform in England (see pp.10–11). Burrell also bought outstanding examples of Elizabethan and Jacobean ceremonial dining ware, symbols of grandeur and wealth in banquet-style dining of this period. Burrell, though usually considered in his expenditure, was willing to spend large sums to acquire these pieces. In 1939, he purchased a magnificent set of three silver-gilt steeple standing cups (see pp.14–15) from the collection of American newspaper magnate William Randolph Hearst (1863–1951), for £3,900, the largest amount he spent on a silver object and one of the biggest single purchases he made during his collecting career.

Opposite: A silver-gilt chalice, 1500–25, purchased by Sir William Burrell in 1937, most likely originally made for use in the ritual of the Eucharist, a part of the Catholic Mass (43.2).

Objects in Focus

In the 1530s, King Henry VIII (1491–1547) broke away from the Roman Catholic Church, declaring himself the Supreme Head of the new Church of England. This Protestant Reformation led to the destruction and seizure of monastic lands and wealth, including silver artefacts. Surviving pre-Reformation ecclesiastical silver is rare. Burrell, however, acquired a pyx in 1948, from his long-term dealer and friend John Hunt (1900–76). The pyx was used as a dish for holding consecrated bread during Catholic Mass.

As Protestant faith grew in England during the sixteenth century, religious silver changed in fashion to reflect Protestant ritual. In the 1560s, Catholic practices, including the belief in transubstantiation – the transforming of bread and wine into the body and blood of Christ during the ritual of the Eucharist – were declared illegal. Chalices for communion were no longer reserved for the clergy and ornately decorated with religious imagery, as in the Catholic tradition. Instead, they took the form of simple standing cups, often decorated with strapwork and arabesque motifs, and were used for communal drinking. Burrell collected several examples of later sixteenth-century chalices; this example has a cover, or paten, designed to keep falling dust or dirt from contaminating the wine. The paten could also be inverted to be used as a dish for communion bread.

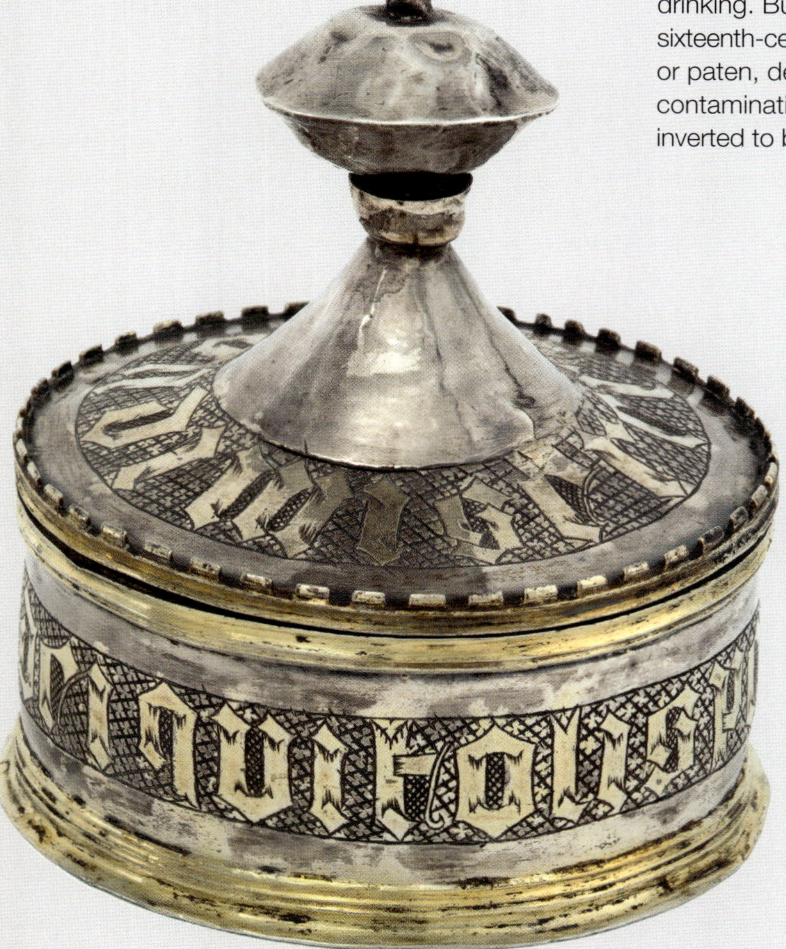

Pyx, 1470–1500
Possibly made in England
Silver, silver gilt
8.7 cm x 8 cm x 7.9 cm
43.133

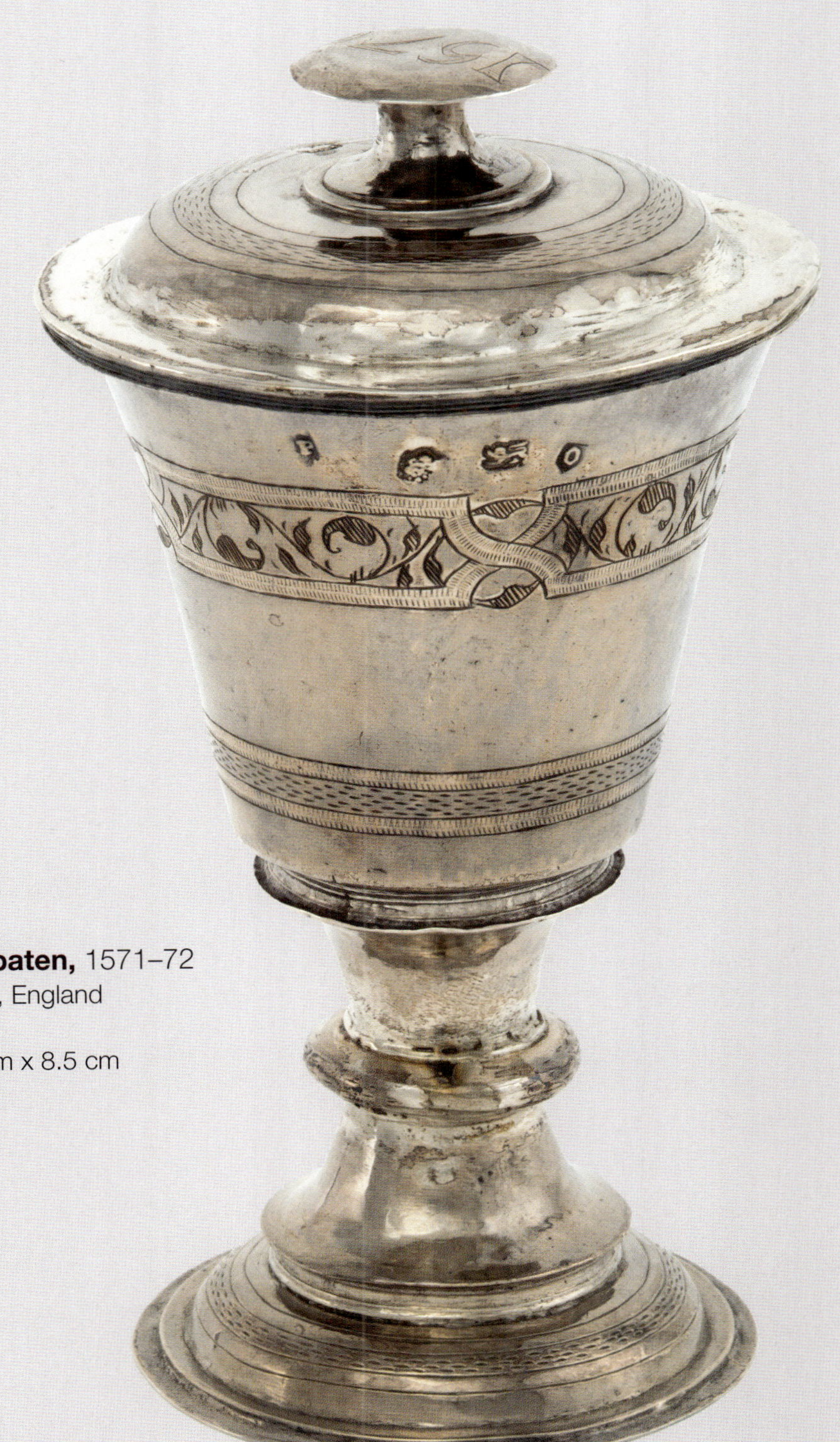

Chalice with paten, 1571–72
Made in London, England
Silver
15.4 cm x 8.6 cm x 8.5 cm
2.8 cm x 6.1 cm
43.6.1, 43.6.2

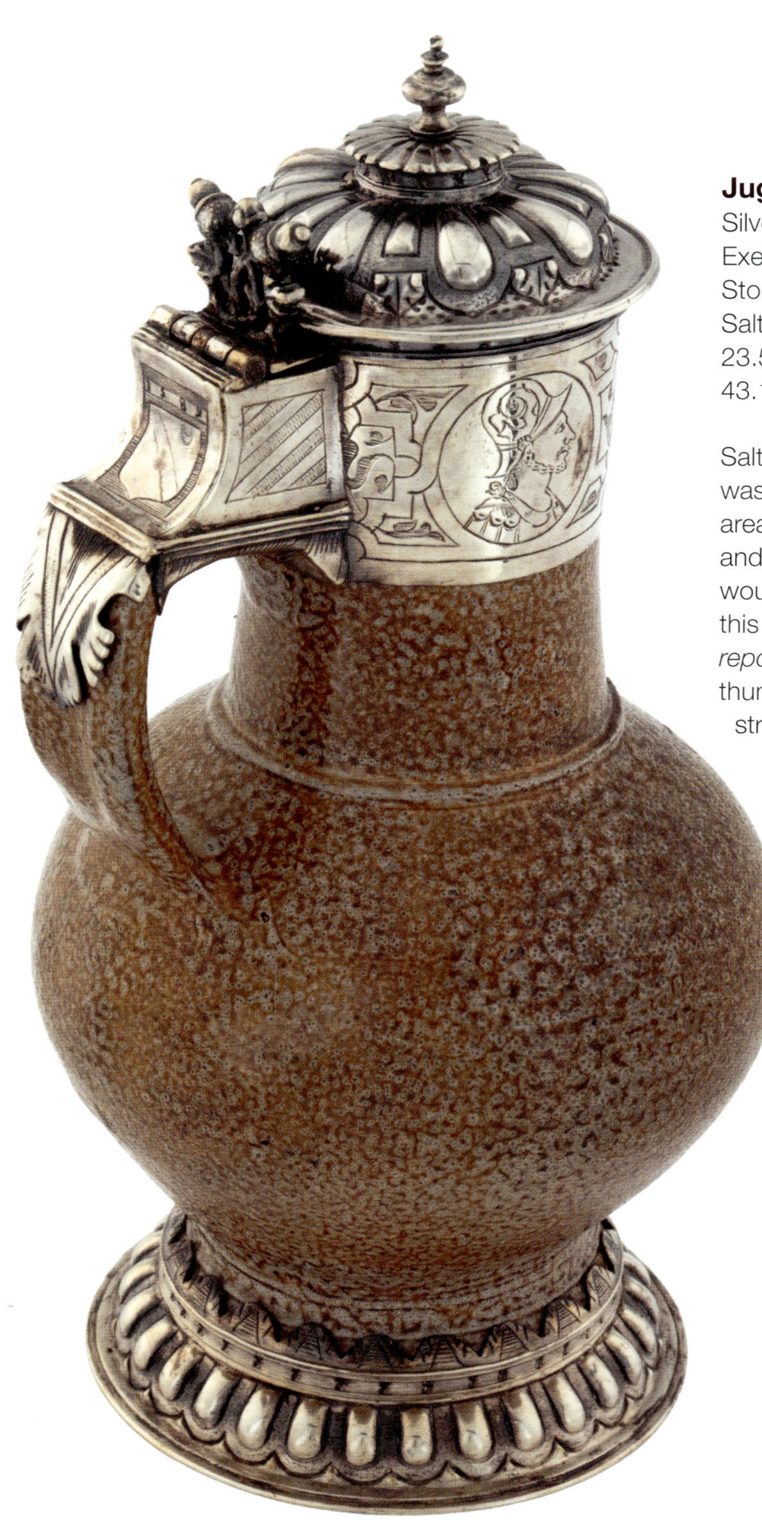

Jug with mounts, 1580–1600
Silver mounts made by Christopher Easton,
Exeter, England
Stone jug made in Germany
Salt-glazed stoneware, silver
23.5 cm x 12.8 cm x 11.8 cm
43.117

Salt-glazed stoneware, known as tigerware,
was imported in vast quantities from the Rhineland
areas of Germany to England during the sixteenth
and seventeenth centuries. Wealthy consumers
would have their stone pots mounted with silver;
this jug is mounted with a silver embossed,
repoussé foot and hinged cover, with an acorn
thumbpiece, and a neck band engraved with
strapwork and three medallions enclosing two
Romanesque-style male and one female
heads. The town of Exeter was a large
importer of German stoneware, and local
goldsmiths often produced silver mount
work. These silver mounts bear the mark
'ESTON' for Christopher Easton, an
Exeter goldsmith active at the end of
the 1500s.

Bell salt, 1603–04
Made in London, England
Silver-gilt
Maker's mark 'TS' in monogram
23.5 cm x 12 cm x 12 cm
43.152

By the early-seventeenth century, salt was still
considered a luxury commodity, displayed on the
dining table in ceremonial silverware like this bell salt,
decorated with chased and *repoussé* strapwork,
hops, gourds, and acanthus foliage. This salt is made
with two tapering sections, which when pulled apart
reveal a sunken bowl to hold the salt. The smaller of
the two sections was for the host, providing them
with a personal supply of salt as a signal to the other
guests of their authority. The large, bottom section
was placed centrally for guests. The domed cap
with pierced finial was used as a pepper-caster.

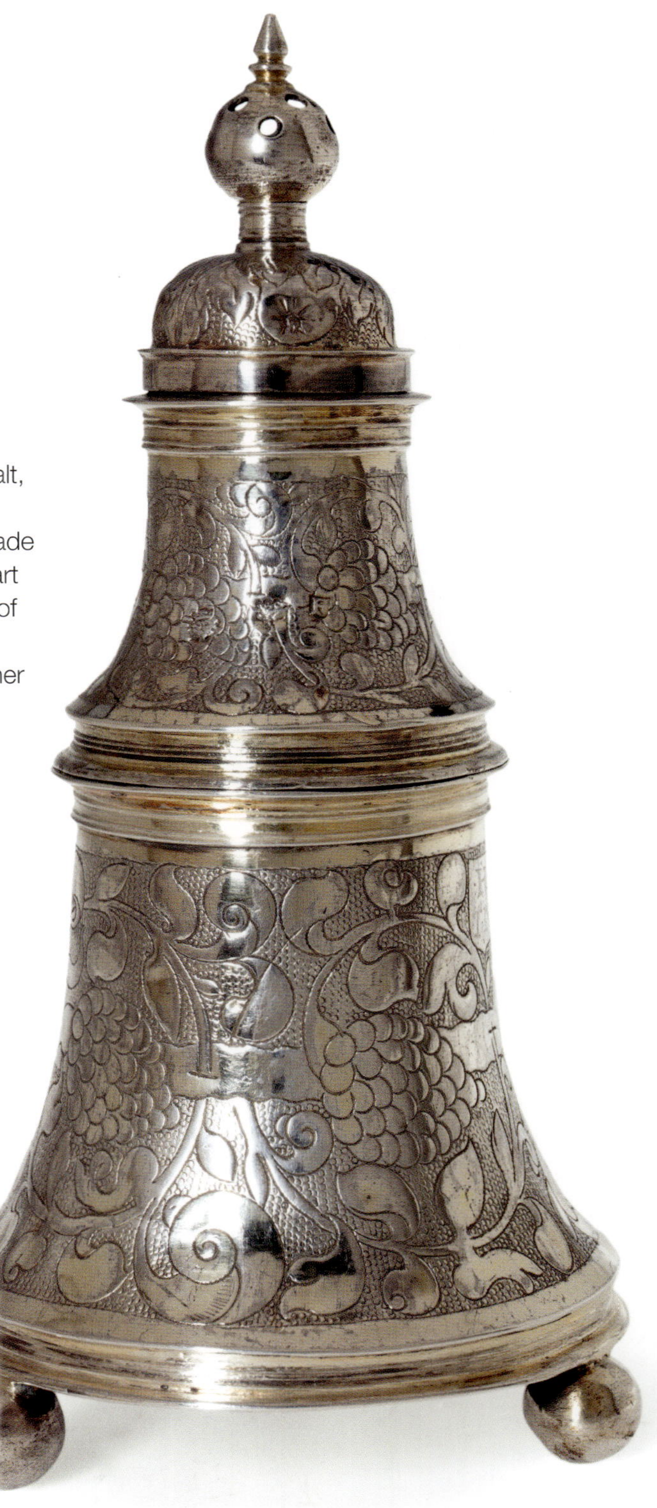

Objects in Focus

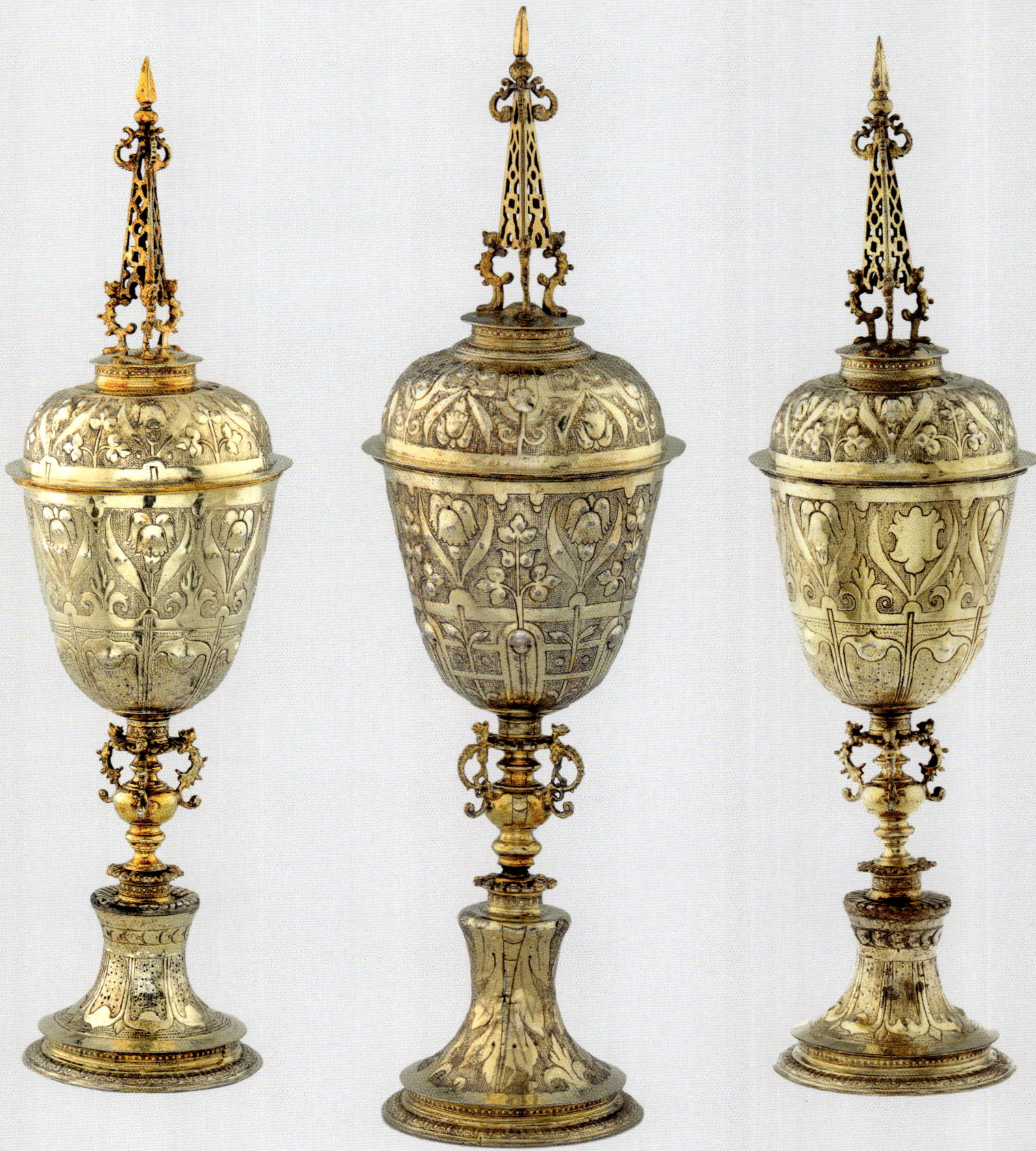

Set of standing cups with steeple covers,
1611–12
Made in London, England
Silver-gilt
45 cm x 13 cm x 13 cm
46 cm x 13 cm x 13 cm
47.5 cm x 14 cm x 14 cm
43.16, 43.17, 43.18

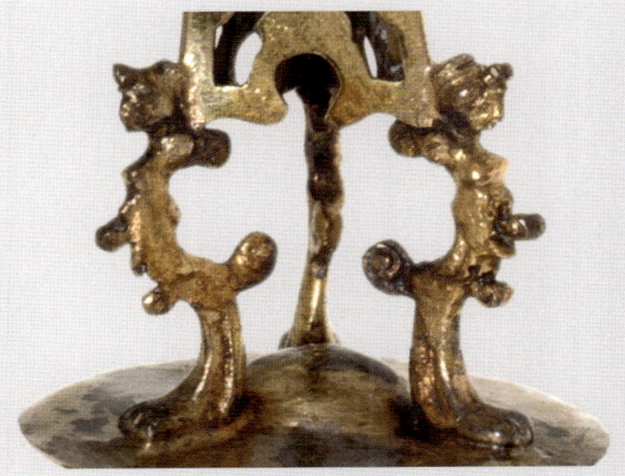

Detail of caryatid figures supporting the 'steeple' finials.

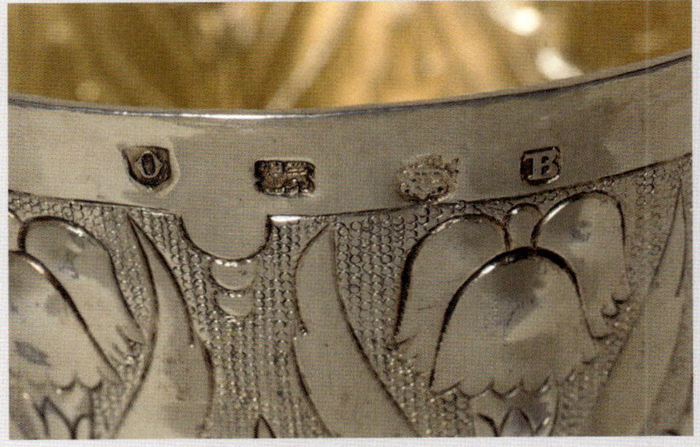

It is extremely rare for a set of three steeple cups to survive. These were almost certainly made as a set, as each bear the maker's mark of 'TB' on the bowls and covers.

This superb set of three standing cups and covers is highly decorated with chased and embossed patterns of foliage, carnations, and tulips, each stem ornamented with handle-like scrolls, embellished with female monster heads. The name 'steeple' is given to cups of this design after the tall spire-like finials decorating the domed covers. These finials, also known as 'obelisks' or 'pinnacles', would have been understood during the late-sixteenth and early-seventeenth centuries as symbols of greatness and power. The 'steeple' finials on these cups are triangular, with pierced open work, supported by caryatid figures.

Although made of silver, the gold colour was created through the process of gilding, creating silver-gilt. A mixture of mercury and molten gold was applied to the finished cups, and then heated. The heat dissolved the mercury, leaving a fine layer of the gold colour behind on the surface.

Standing cups and covers of this type were fashionable during the late-sixteenth and early-seventeenth centuries and considered English in origin and design. Steeple cups were commonly used as part of a grand buffet of plate – a spectacular display of silver or gold tableware, placed at the side of the dining table. Often cups and plate on the buffet were used only for display, signifying to guests the owner's wealth.

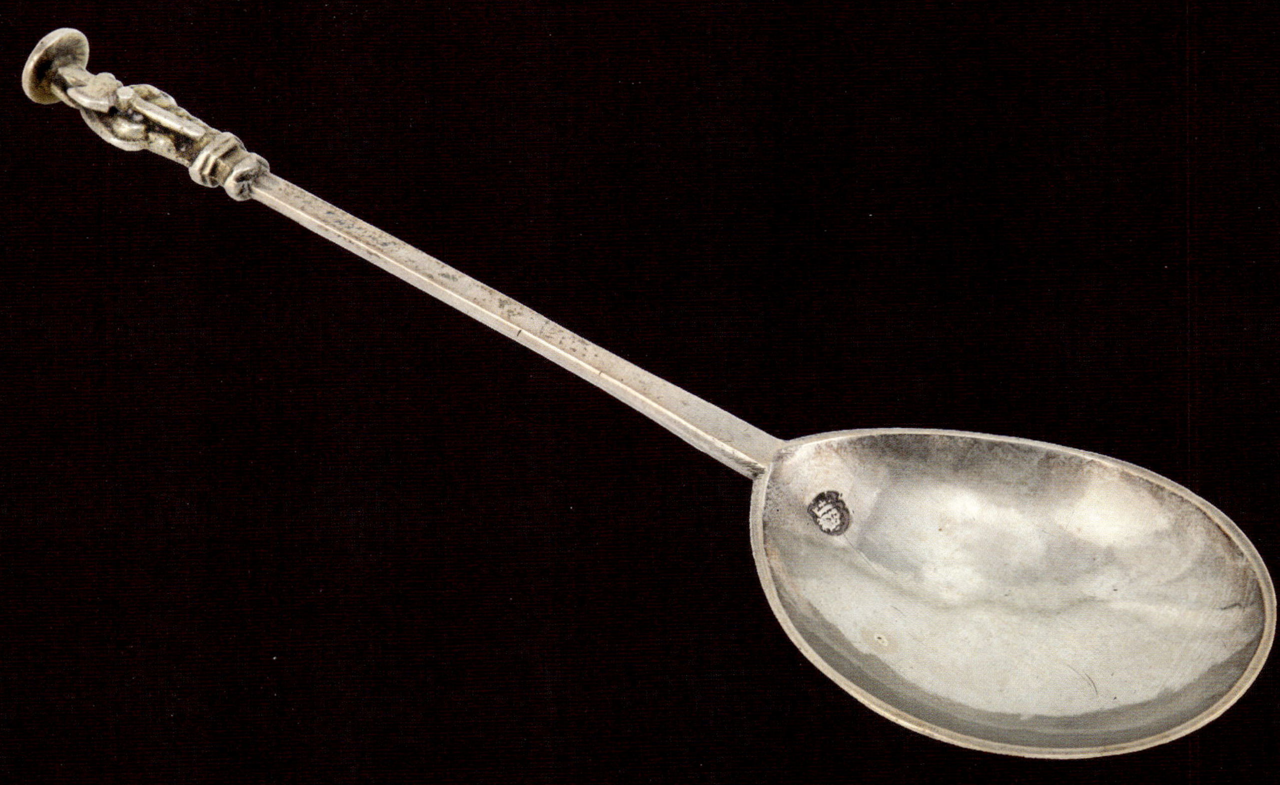

Apostle spoon, 1636–37
Made by Richard Crosse, London, England
Silver-gilt
1.5 cm x 5.1 cm x 11 cm
43.220

This silver-gilt spoon with egg-shaped bowl has a tapering stem terminating in a decorative knop in the form of a bearded apostle figure. By the sixteenth century, silver spoons of this type, known as apostle spoons, were given as baptismal gifts from wealthy godparents to be used by the newly christened child throughout its lifetime. Flatware such as spoons and knives were personal items, the individual bringing their own set to each meal. The tiny apostle terminations are identified by the objects or symbols they hold; this figure, depicted with a nimbus or halo, holds a halberd for St Matthew.

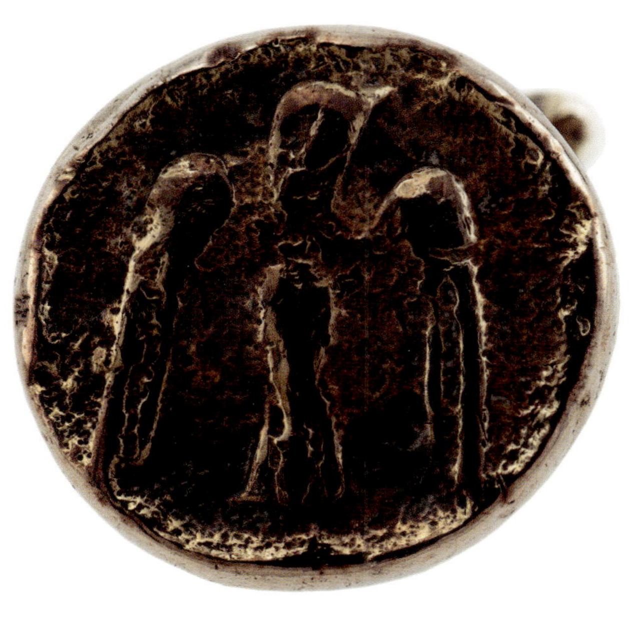

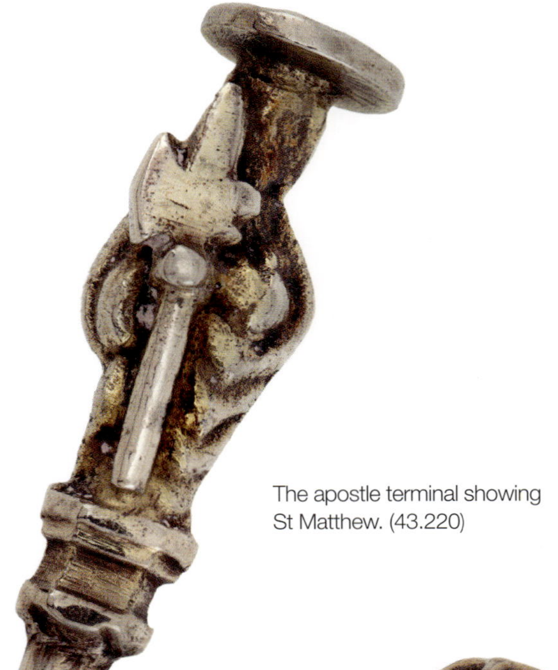

The top of the halo on the St Matthew apostle terminal has a representation of a flying dove, a symbol of the Holy Spirit in Christianity. (43.220)

The apostle terminal showing St Matthew. (43.220)

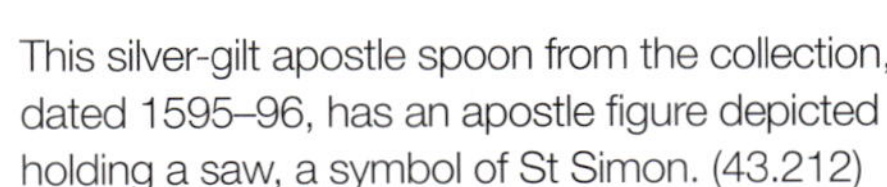

This silver-gilt apostle spoon from the collection, dated 1595–96, has an apostle figure depicted holding a saw, a symbol of St Simon. (43.212)

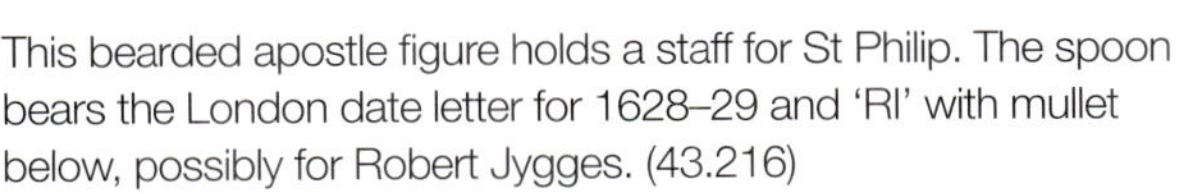

This bearded apostle figure holds a staff for St Philip. The spoon bears the London date letter for 1628–29 and 'RI' with mullet below, possibly for Robert Jygges. (43.216)

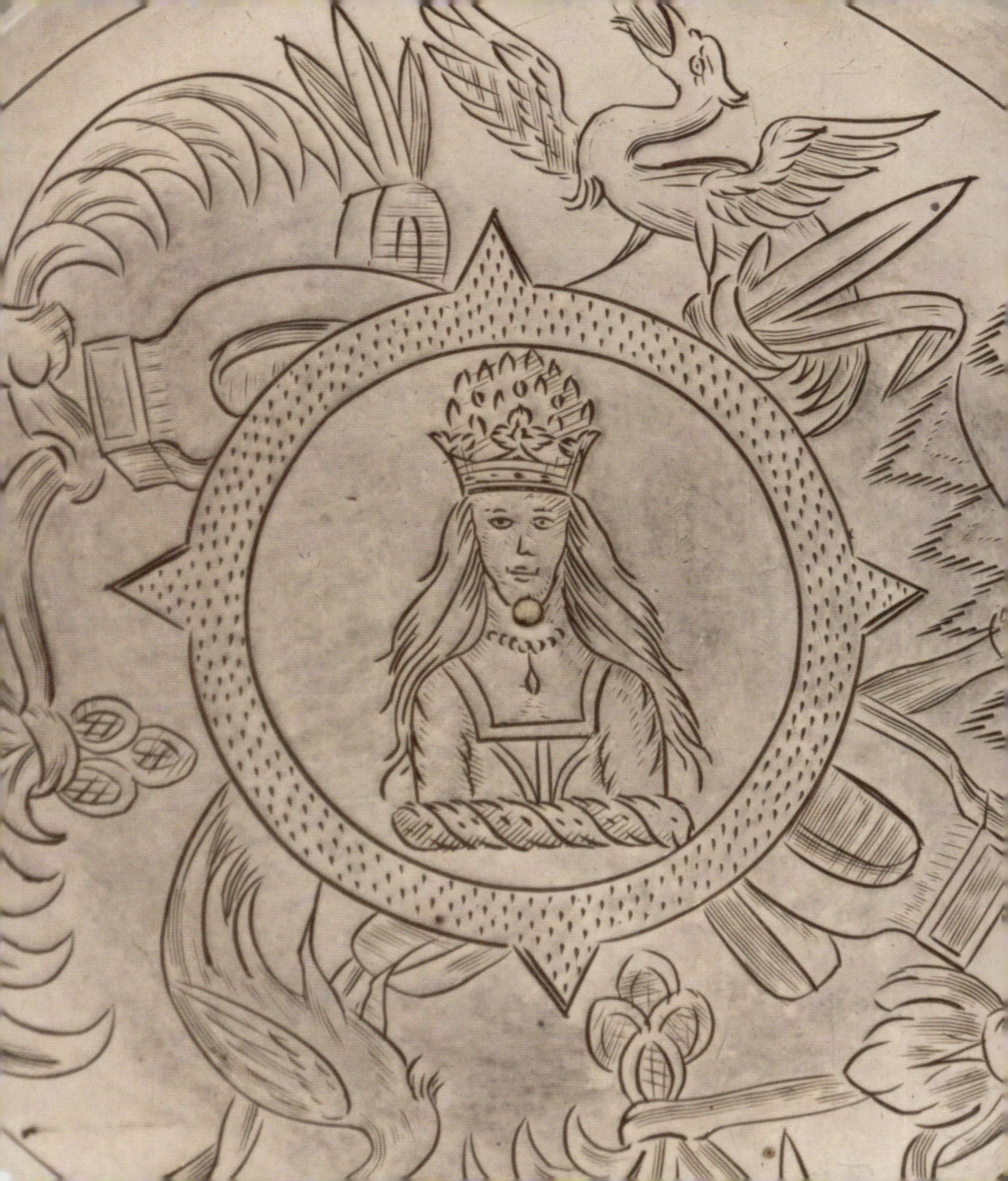

Domestic Silver

Silver production and consumption in the seventeenth century was influenced by the changing political and economic landscape. During the 1640s, clashes between King Charles I (1600–49) and Parliament led to civil war in England, with battles taking place on English soil between the armies of the monarchy, the Royalists, and the government, the Parliamentarians. Churches, universities, civic institutions, and wealthy individuals surrendered their household plate to show loyalty and generate funds required by either king or parliament. Ultimately, the armies of Charles I were defeated by the Parliamentarian forces led by Oliver Cromwell (1599–1658), leading to the execution of the king in 1649, and the establishment of the Commonwealth – government rule of England and Wales by the House of Commons.

This period of political instability is often wrongly described as leading to the mass destruction of English silver objects from before the seventeenth century. However, silver production continued throughout the mid-seventeenth century, and limited representation of sixteenth and early-seventeenth century silver was more likely due to patrons commissioning silversmiths to melt down old plate and rework the silver into new fashionable items.

The Restoration of the English monarchy with King Charles II (1630–85) in 1660 led to a renewed interest in commissions of silver plate in new fashions, influenced by the emerging Baroque styles popular on the European continent. Luxury goods of silver were now attainable, not just for the aristocracy or church, but also for the emerging affluent elite of merchants, landowners, and gentry of the late-seventeenth century. The trade in domestic silver soared with increased numbers of silversmiths establishing independent workshops and selling their silver at retail, commissions being created to the patron's specific tastes and chosen using pattern books detailing fashionable designs.

In the seventeenth century, the fashion for public, communal grand dinners in great halls fell away. Instead, dining moved into smaller, intimate private rooms, reserved for only a few guests. The Burrells' collection of seventeenth-century silver demonstrates the broad range of domestic silver objects created during this period, including personal items like porringers, tankards, toilet services, and snuff boxes.

Opposite: Engraving on salver, 1693–94, by John Ruslen, London, England, 43.78 (detail; see also p.34).

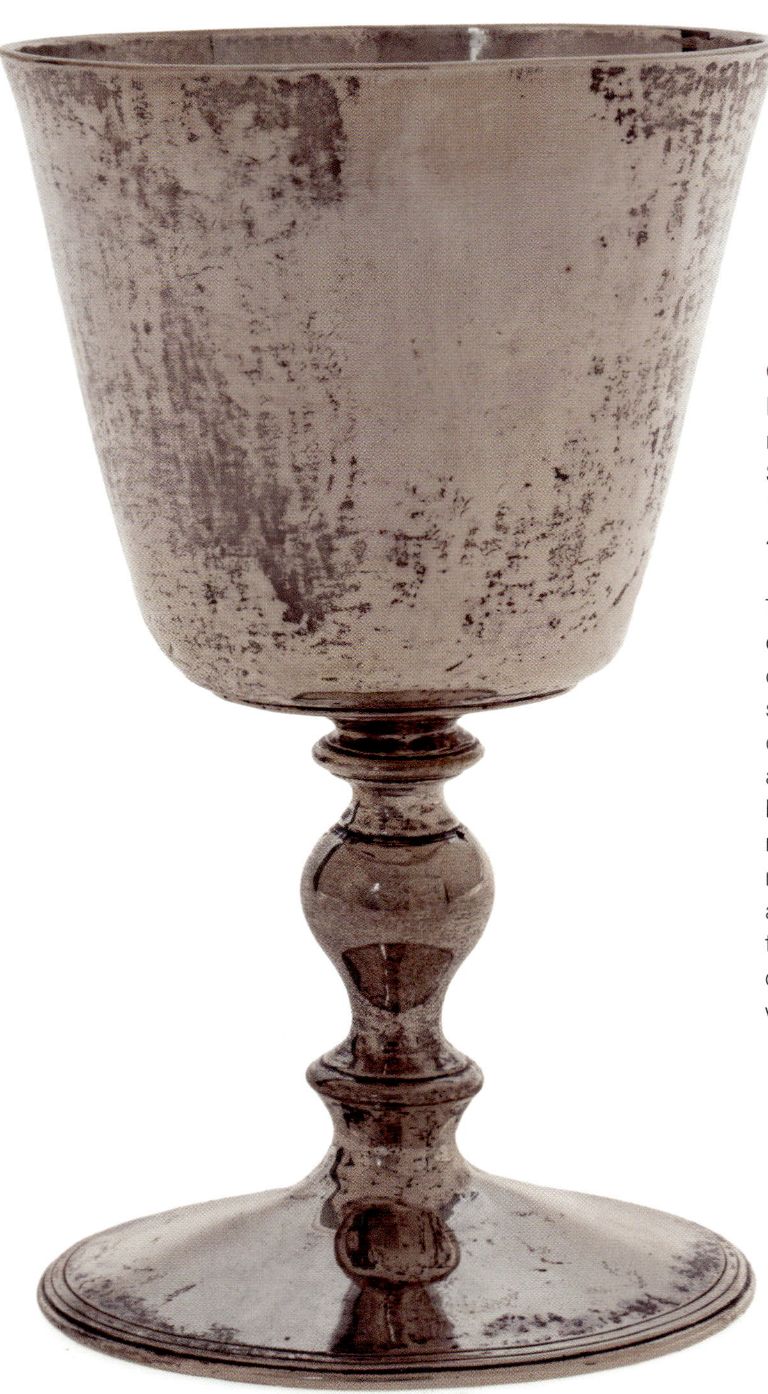

Goblet, 1641–42
Made in London, England,
marked with 'IH' over mullet
Silver
16.5 cm x 9.1 cm x 9.1 cm
43.28

This is a rare example of an early-seventeenth
century silver goblet created on the cusp
of the English Civil War (1642–51), which
survived the melting of silver plate prevalent
during this period of unrest. The goblet has
a straight-sided bowl, supported by a
baluster stem and domed circular foot with
reeded rim. Baluster stems, identified by their
rounded bulbous vase-like shape, became
a popular form for silver standing cups of
this period. By the end of the seventeenth
century, the fashion for silver goblets for wine
was replaced with glass drinking vessels.

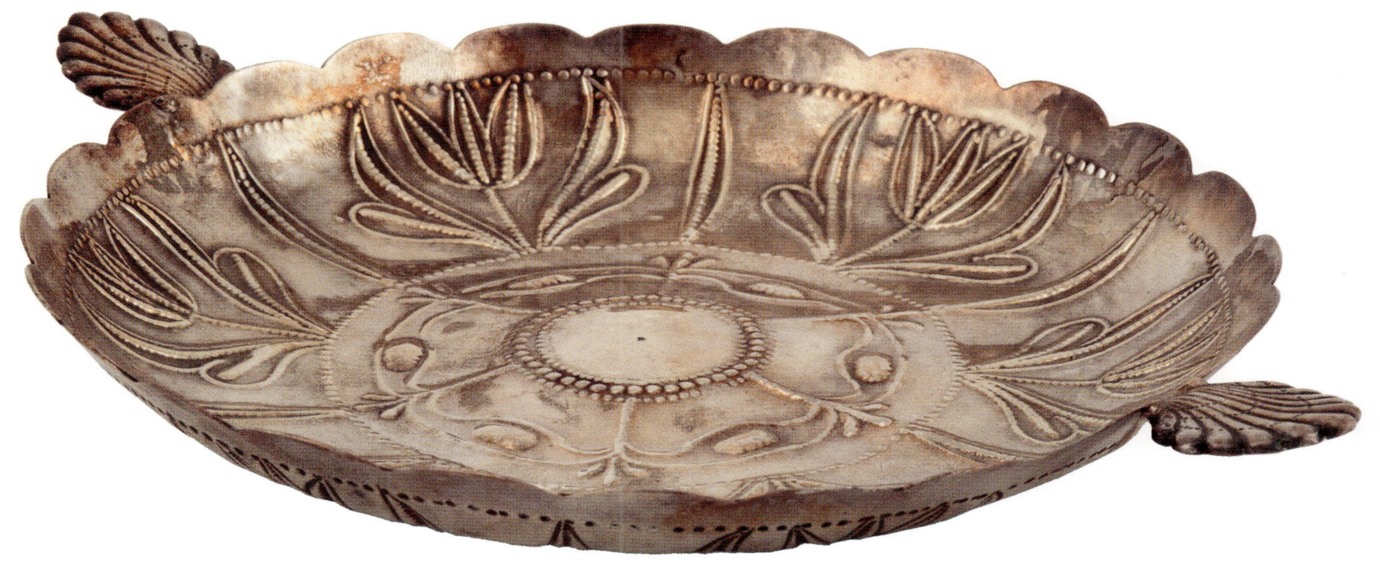

Sweetmeat dish, 1655–56
Made by Nicholas Wollaston, London, England
Silver
3 cm x 22.6 cm x 17.4 cm
43.82

Dishes of this shape and decoration were popular in the seventeenth century for the serving of sugared sweetmeats. This dish has a shallow bowl with a wavy edge and two shell-shaped handles. The raised relief decoration of flowers and foliage was stamped on the reverse with punches – round-edged chisels used to push the metal outwards. This technique is known as *repoussé* from the French for 'pushed up'. Before punching, the dish would be secured into pitch, a soft putty material, providing support to the metal when being pushed into its new shape. This style of two-handled punched dish ceased production by the late-seventeenth century.

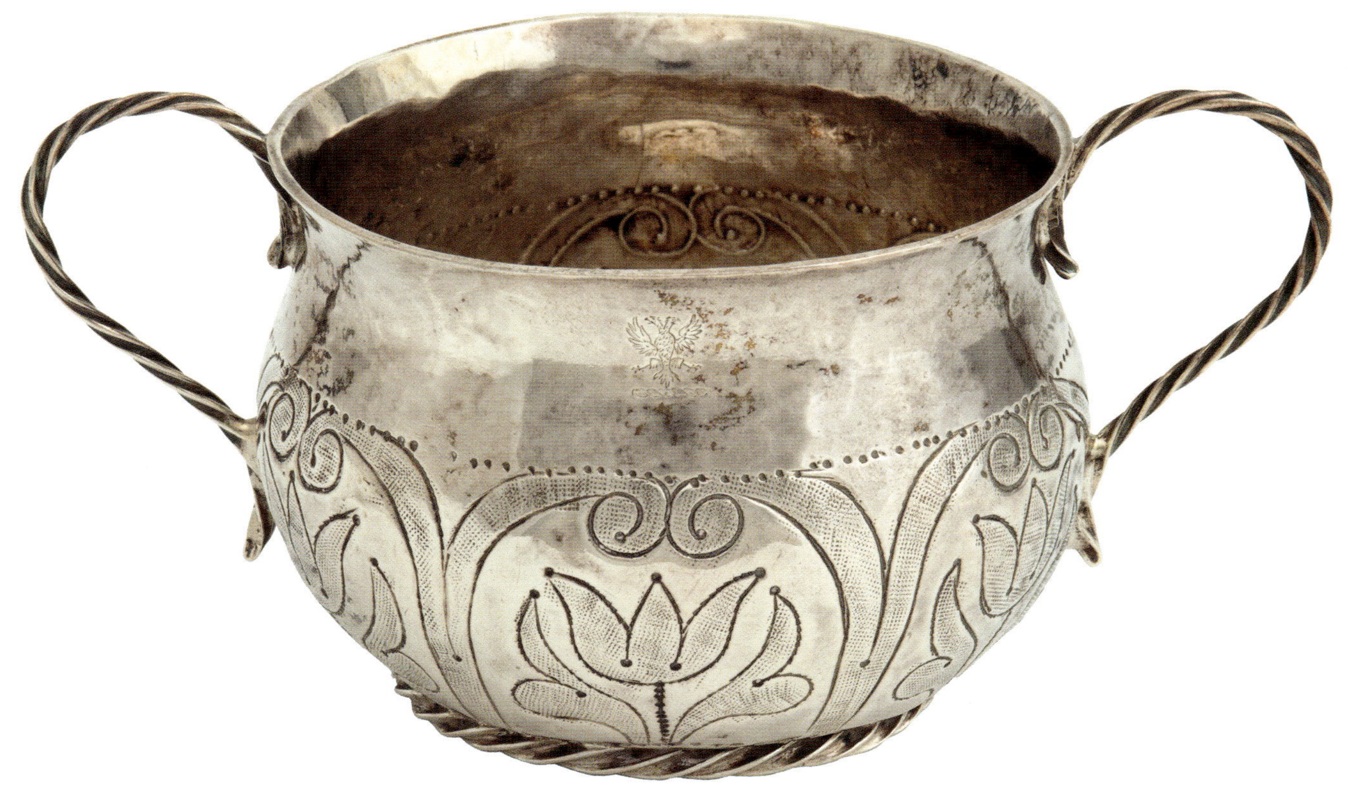

Porringer, 1656–57
Possibly made by Christopher Shaw, London, England
Silver
7.8 cm x 16 cm x 10.2 cm
43.95

Porringers were common throughout the seventeenth century and were used for eating liquid foods such as stews and broths. Silver porringers commonly have one or two handles, cast separately, and soldered onto the side, providing a place to grip the bowl. These types of bowls are sometimes referred to as 'caudle cups'; caudle being a restorative thick sweet alcoholic drink served to women after childbirth. This porringer has a globular bowl, with punched decoration of flowering tulip plants. The two scrolling handles and foot are made from silver cable which has been twisted to create a spiral effect.

Puritan spoon, 1662–63
Made by Jeremy Johnson, London, England
Silver
2.1 cm x 4.9 cm x 18.2 cm
43.206

This spoon features a flattened stem tapering towards an egg-shaped bowl. Spoons of this plain decoration are often referred to as Puritan spoons. Silver created in the Commonwealth of England (1649–60) reflected Protestant Puritan ideals, including the rejection of elaborate decoration. This spoon is marked with the London date letter for 1662–63, indicating that spoons of this type were still made after the restoration of the monarchy in 1660. The stem has the maker's mark 'II' with pellet between and mullet below, for Jeremy Johnson, a specialist spoon maker working in London during the mid-seventeenth century.

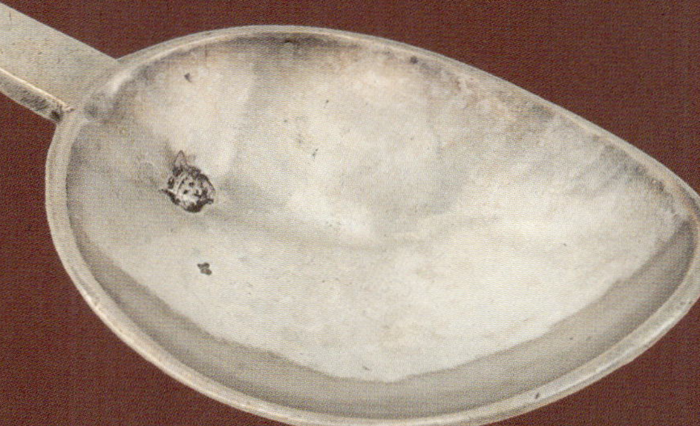

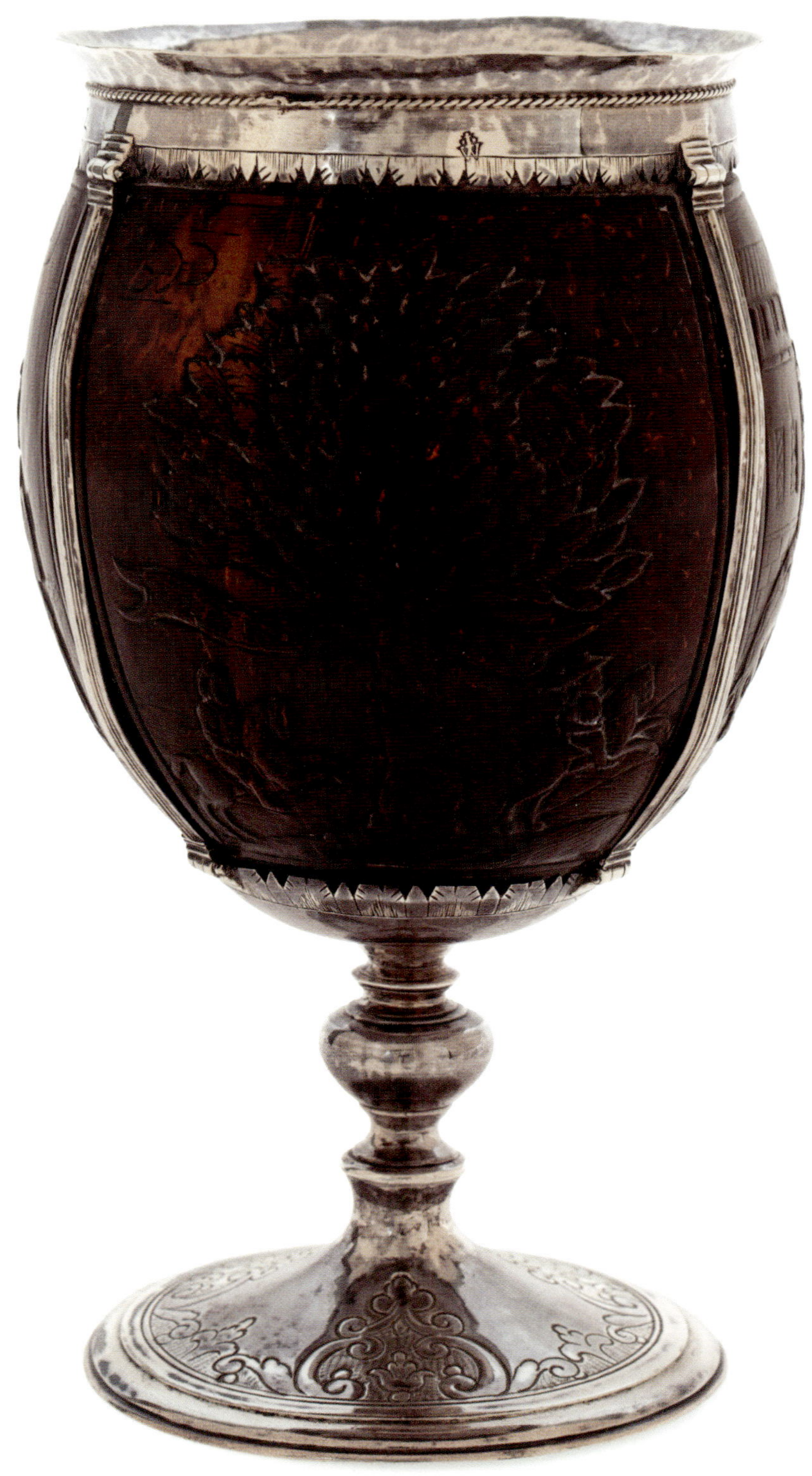

Silver mounted coconut cup carved with Charles II's Flight After the Battle of Worcester, 1625–75

Made in England
Coconut, silver mounts
18.9 cm x 9.5 cm x 9.3 cm
43.21

Natural specimens of shells, minerals, and coconuts were valued as highly exotic curiosities in the sixteenth and seventeenth centuries. These treasured collectables were often mounted with precious metals for display. This coconut, transformed into a standing cup, has silver mounts, and foot, with rim engraved 'G//S/I' and dated '1662'.

Coconuts were imported during the sixteenth century from South America and the West Indies. They were prized for their supposed healing powers. It was believed that drinking from a coconut protected you from poison. The value increased if carved with scenes of religion, mythology, or commemorative events. The coconut of this cup is divided into three sections by silver bands. Each section is carved with a scene of the escape of King Charles II (1630–85) after his defeat at the Battle of Worcester on 3 September 1651. After the battle, Charles fled from Parliamentarian forces, travelling in disguise. In October, he sailed to France where he remained exiled for nine years. Charles was restored to the throne in 1660 leading to a surge of royal memorabilia celebrating his return. Scenes from the dramatic escape of 1651, as seen on this coconut cup, were a common decorative motif to celebrate the Restoration of the monarchy. The most celebrated motif, known as the 'Royal Oak', showed Charles II hiding in an oak tree at Boscobel House, Shropshire, to escape Parliamentary forces.

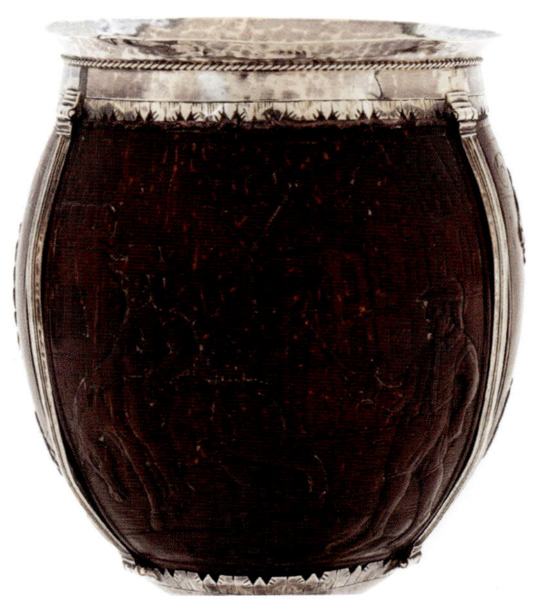

Disguised as a servant, Charles II on horseback is accompanied to Moseley Old Hall, Staffordshire, on 7 September 1651 by Humphrey Penderel, a mill worker.

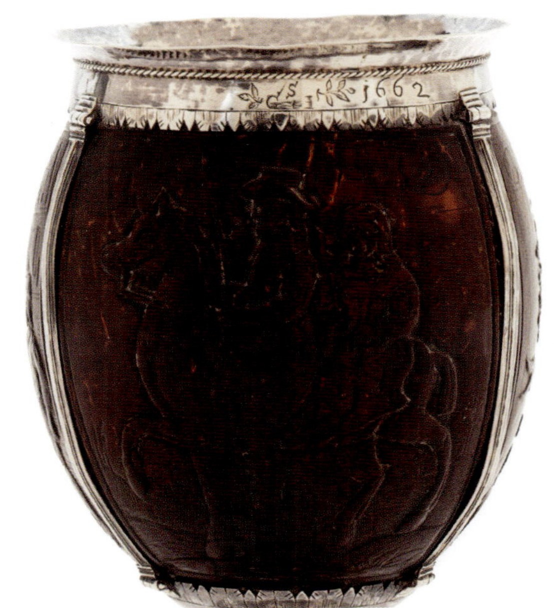

Charles II disguised himself as the servant of Jane Lane of Bentley Hall, accompanying her on her journey to Bristol, where he could catch a ship to the safety of France.

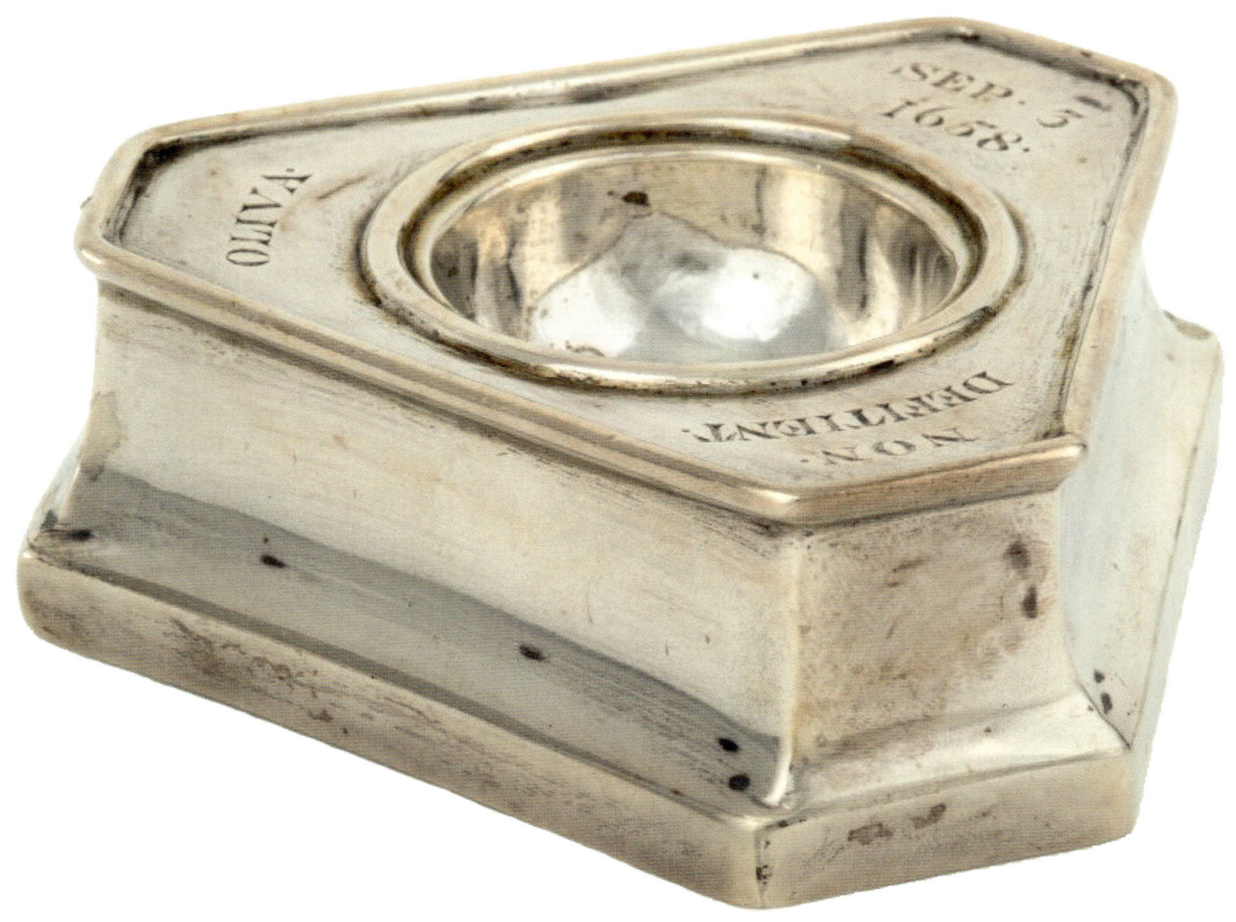

One of a set of trencher salts, 1669–70,
with spoons, 1713–14
Trencher salts made by Lawrence Coles, London,
England
Silver
3.3 cm x 8.8 cm x 9.8 cm
9.2 cm x 2.3 cm x 0.8 cm
43.153.1, 43.153.2

By the seventeenth century, the large singular standing salt was replaced by multiple smaller salt dishes known as trencher salts. A trencher salt was placed by each individual diner's plate or shared, one between two. This is one of a set of four silver trencher salts sunk with a round bowl in a triangular stand with chamfered corners. The salt sat in the rounded bowl and was lifted out with a knife or spoon.

Each salt is inscribed with the phrase 'NON DEFITIENT OLIVA SEP. 3 1658' translating to '[They] shall not be deprived of an olive tree'. This phrase commemorated the death of Oliver Cromwell, who died on 3 September 1658. Cromwell ruled the British Isles as Lord Protector from 1653 until his death, upon

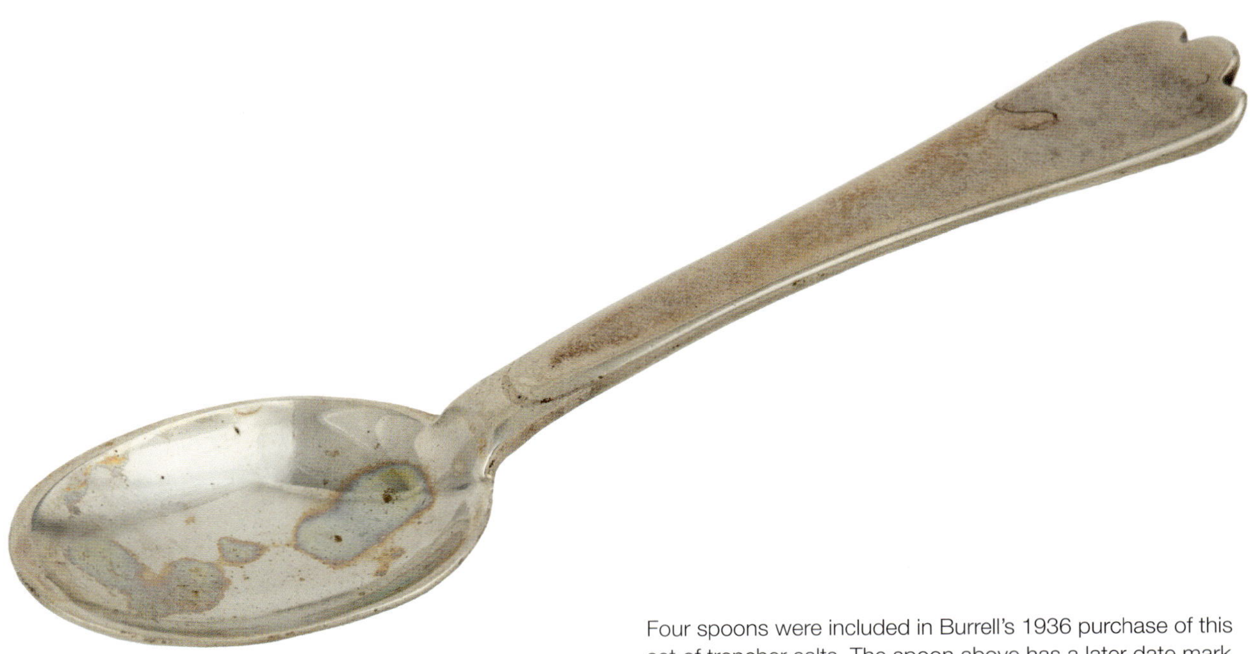

Four spoons were included in Burrell's 1936 purchase of this set of trencher salts. The spoon above has a later date mark than the salts (1713–14), indicating the set of spoons is not original, possibly produced as later replacements.

which his son, Richard Cromwell (1626–1712), succeeded him in the role. The 'olive tree' referred to Cromwell and the knowledge that, despite his death, the people of Britain would be ruled by a new 'tree', Cromwell's son, Richard.

Richard Cromwell renounced his position in 1659, and by 1660 King Charles II was restored to the throne. As this salt was made nine years after the end of the Protectorate, it is possible they were commissioned to commemorate Cromwell's rule and potential opposition to the Restoration of the monarchy.

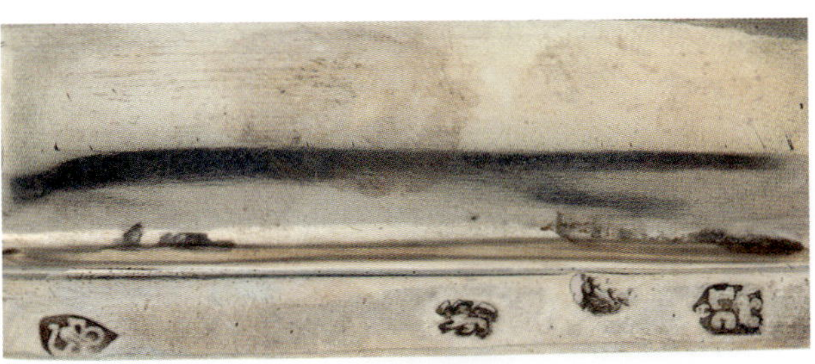

Marks on trencher salt: leopard's head crowned, lion passant, London date letter for 1669–70, maker's mark 'LC', crown and crescent, for Lawrence Coles, a London silversmith active from 1667–1720.

Pair of candlesticks, 1671–72
Made in London, England, marked 'IH' and 'S'
crowned (Robert Smythier)
Silver gilt
22.4 cm x 12.8 cm x 12.9 cm
22.2 cm x 12.9 cm x 13.1 cm
43.173, 43.174

Candlesticks with square bases and column stems
became fashionable during the reign of Charles II.
These silver-gilt candlesticks have acanthus leaf
ornamentation, springing from a square acanthus
leaf platform. The square base is decorated with
cut-card work; the foliage designs were cut from
a sheet of silver and then soldered to the base.
Whilst the stem was raised from a sheet of silver, it
is probable that the heavily ornamented foot was
cast from moulds, allowing the silversmith to make
multiple versions. As casting required more silver
than raising, objects produced in this way were
more expensive for the owner. The candlesticks are
punched with different makers' marks; one with 'IH',
the other with 'S' crowned, for Robert Smythier, a
London silversmith working from 1660–89.

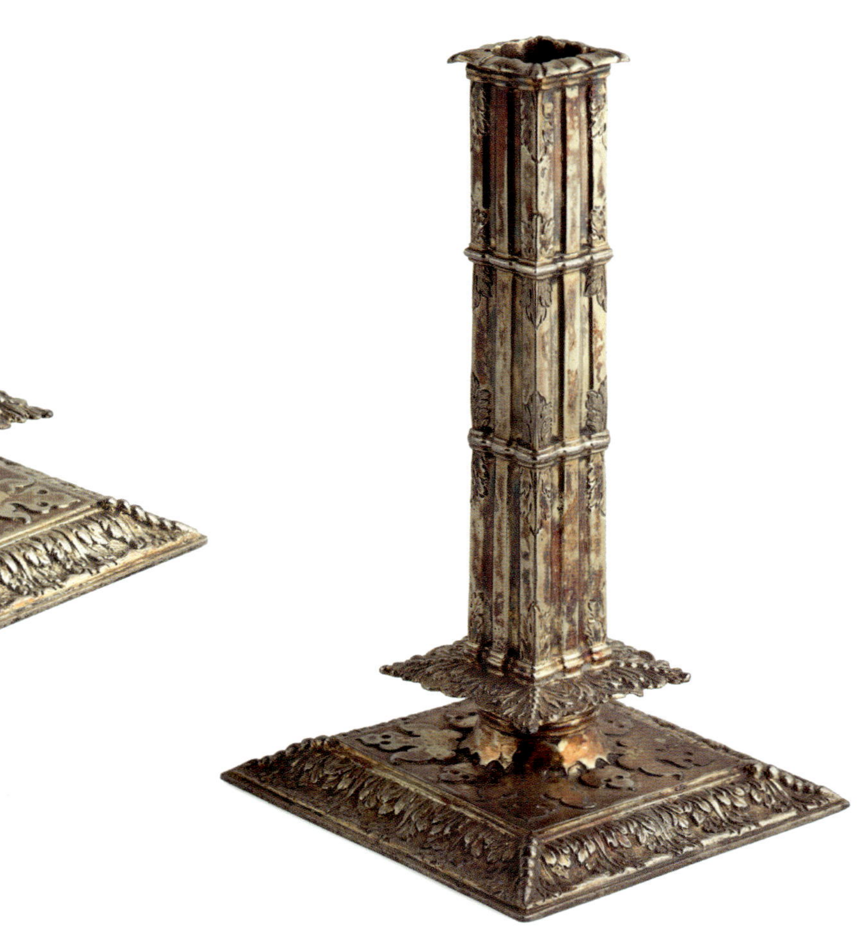

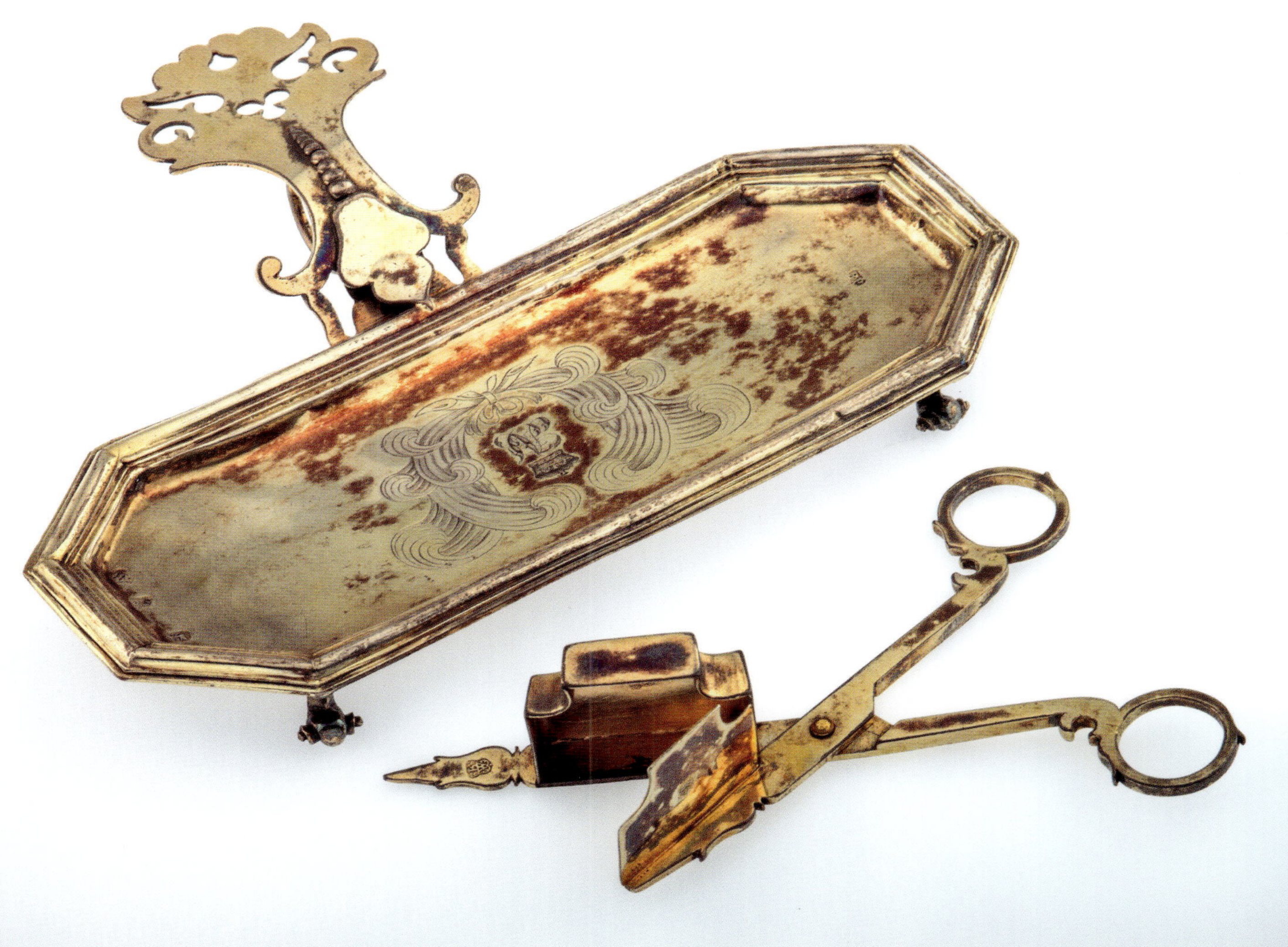

Snuffers with tray, engraved with conjoined cypher 'A F' under ducal coronet, 1680–81
Made in London, England, tray marked with 'BP' and snuffers marked with 'B' over 'W'
4 cm x 24.1 cm x 19.9 cm
4 cm x 6.1 cm x 18.7 cm
43.179.1, 43.179.2

Snuffers were used to trim the burnt candle wicks. The blades of these silver scissor snuffers finish with a flat pressing plate and a box which fit together when the blades are closed. The burnt wick would be positioned between the open snuffer blades, and clamped shut, the blades trimmed the wick while the pressing plate swept the burnt wick and melted wax, known as 'snuff', into the compartment. These snuffers are paired with a tray to catch any stray flakes of wax and rest the snuffers on when not in use.

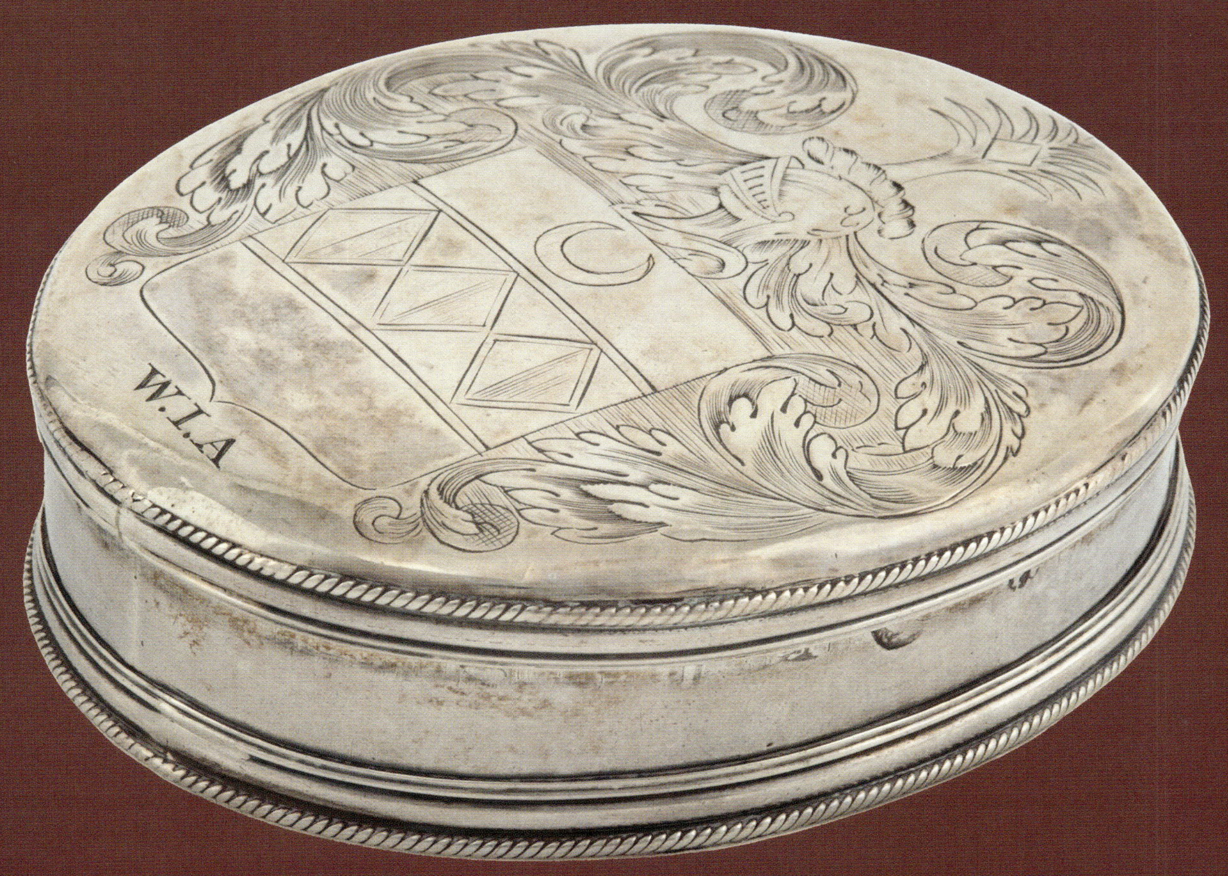

Tobacco box, 1685–86
Made in London, England
Silver
2.5 cm x 8.8 cm x 7.5 cm
43.138

The taking of tobacco grew in popularity amongst the wealthy European elite during the seventeenth century. Tobacco was predominantly grown in British-owned American colonies, the crop harvested by enslaved African people forced to work on tobacco plantations. Oval silver boxes were fashionable in the seventeenth century to store tobacco, because they were small enough to slip into a pocket, and the use of silver denoted the luxury contents. It is possible this box stored snuff, which is powdered tobacco consumed by sniffing. Silver tobacco boxes were often personalized; this box is engraved with the coat of arms of the Feilding family, who were granted the English peerage of the Earl of Denbigh in the early-seventeenth century.

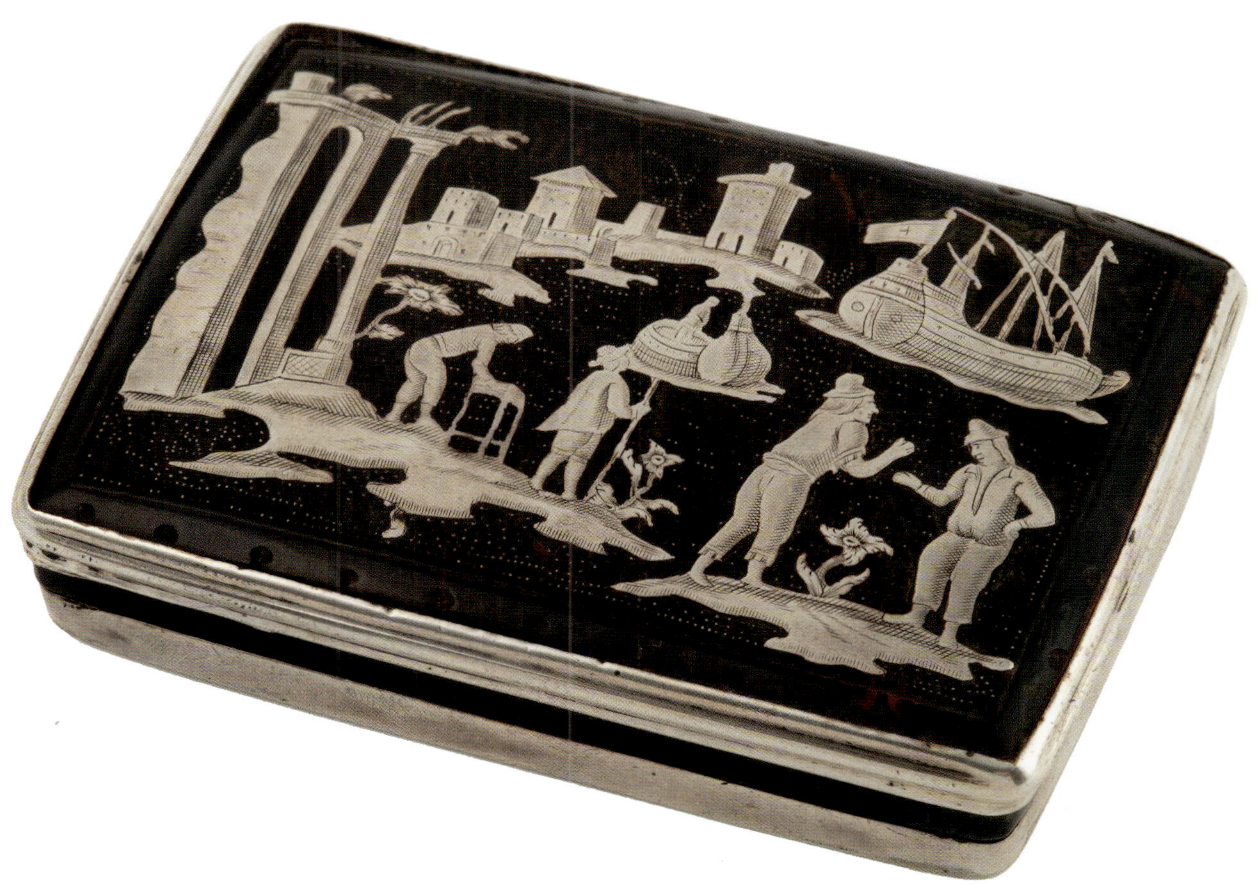

Tortoiseshell box with inlaid silver piqué,

1675–1700
Made in London, England
Tortoiseshell, silver
1.7 cm x 7.8 cm x 5.9 cm
3.28

All of the tortoiseshell items in the Burrell Collection were made
before the 1977 ban on the international trade of tortoiseshell.

Tortoiseshell – the translucent, mottled material
created from the shells of Hawksbill turtles, hunted
in the growing British colonies of the Caribbean –
was regarded as an exotic commodity in the
seventeenth century. The luxury status of the
tortoiseshell in this snuff box is elevated using
silver *piqué* decoration; the inlaying of small pins
of silver into the tortoiseshell to create patterns.
This box, with hinged lid and silver mounts, has
a *piqué* decoration depicting a coastal landscape
with ship, boat and four figures on the shoreline.
Tiny points of silver *piqué* inlay are used to create
the rolling waves of water.

Tankard with Hasluck coat of arms,

1678–79
Possibly made by John Ruslen, London, England
Silver
21 cm x 23.4 cm x 16.5 cm
43.55

Drinking vessels like tankards are identified by tall cylindrical sides and hinged lids, protecting the drink within. The open trellis thumbpiece on this example allowed the drinker to flip the lid open with their thumb. This tankard is engraved with the Hasluck family coat of arms: chevron ermine between three catherine-wheels. Heraldic engraving grew in popularity during the seventeenth century, and it was typically used to denote ownership of the object or honour patrons. A common decorative motif was scrolling mantling surrounding the armorials; plumed ostrich feathers, as seen on this tankard, were fashionable in the late-seventeenth century.

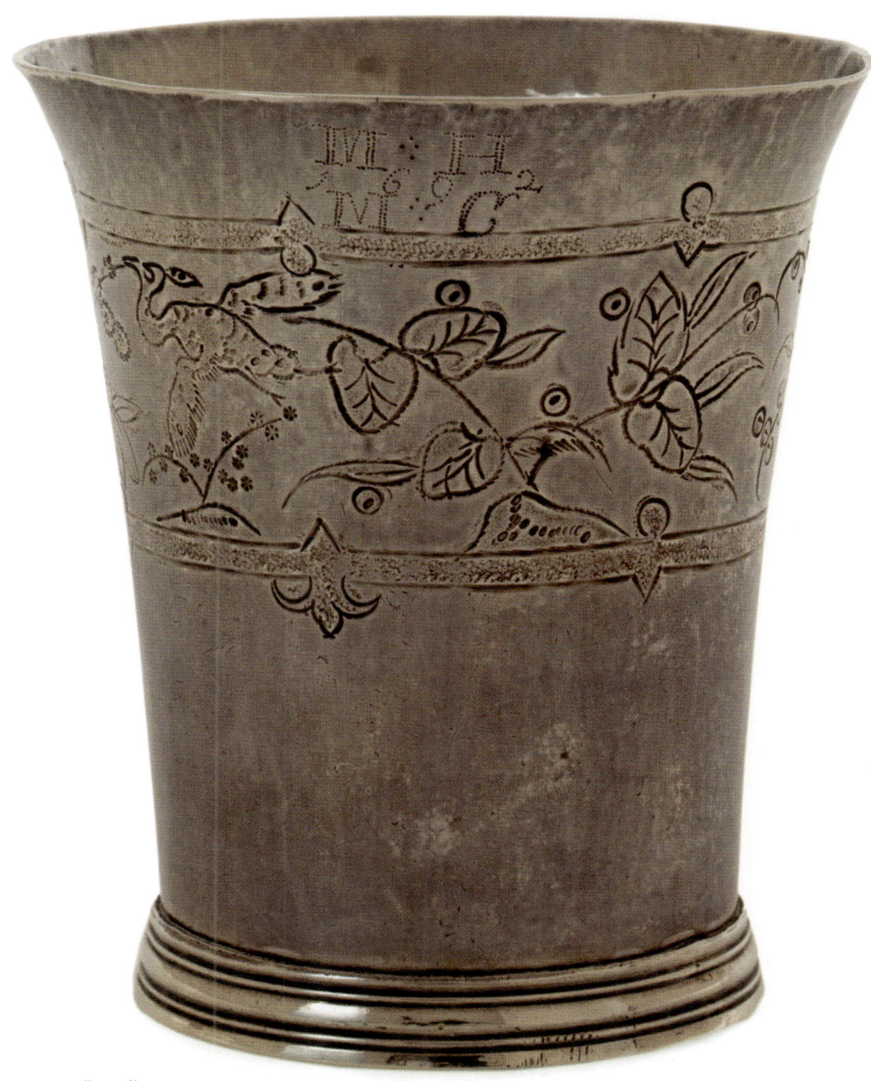

Beaker, 1692–93
Made in London, England
Silver
9.2 cm x 8.1 cm x 8.1 cm
43.25

This beaker, with straight body, spreading lip, and reeded foot, is decorated with birds, foliage, and berries, in Chinoiserie style – a romanticized European-created decoration based on artistic motifs and culture from China. Chinoiserie designs of landscapes, flowers, and birds flat-chased on silver were highly fashionable in the late-seventeenth century, as seen on this beaker. The lip is pricked with 'MH' and 'MC' and '1692'. Silver was frequently gifted to commemorate a new marriage and the pricked decoration is probably the initials of the wedded couple and the date of their union.

Pair of salvers, 1693–94
Made by John Ruslen, London, England
Silver, engraved with the crest of the
Mercers' Company
15.1 cm x 10.6 cm x 10.6 cm
15.7 cm x 10.7 mm x 10.7 mm
43.77, 43.78

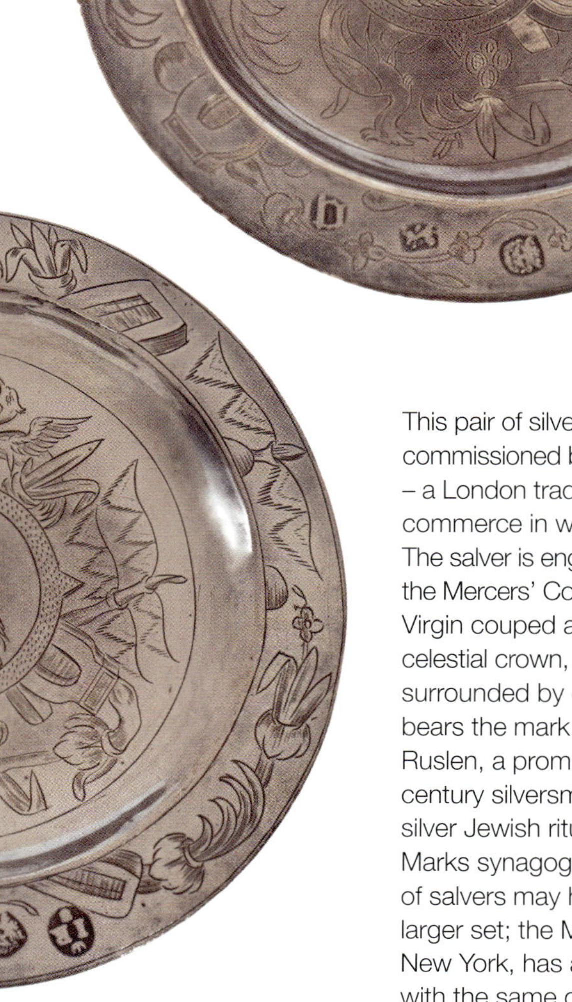

This pair of silver salvers was probably
commissioned by the Mercers' Company
– a London trade association, supporting
commerce in wool, and luxury fabrics.
The salver is engraved with the crest of
the Mercers' Company: a figure of the
Virgin couped at the shoulders, with
celestial crown, within a central roundel,
surrounded by exotic birds. The rim
bears the mark for silversmith John
Ruslen, a prominent late-seventeenth
century silversmith, known for creating
silver Jewish ritual objects for the Bevis
Marks synagogue, in London. This pair
of salvers may have formed part of a
larger set; the Metropolitan Museum,
New York, has a set of four salvers
with the same decoration and marks.

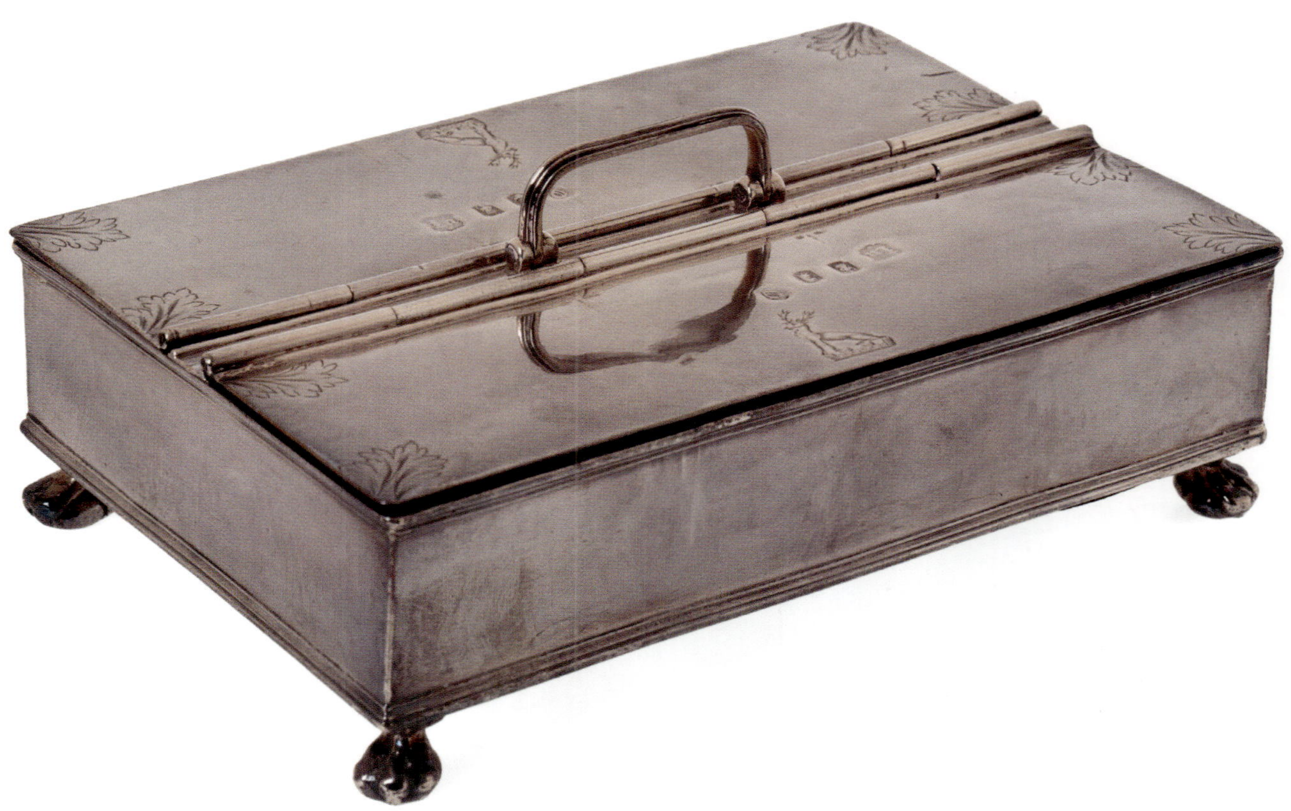

Inkstand, 1699–1700
Made by William Lukin, London, England
Silver
7.3 cm x 17.2 cm x 11.2 cm
43.269

Double-sided silver inkstands, like this example, are often known as 'Treasury' inkstands. In 1686, an order of a 'double standish' (inkstand) was made for the British Treasury department, with several examples still surviving today. This oblong inkstand is supported by four claw feet, with a small central handle between two compartments with hinged lids. One compartment held writing pens, while the other contains a glass inkwell with silver top for ink. An additional silver box with perforated top, kept in this compartment, held pounce, a fine sand sprinkled on the paper to absorb any excess wet ink.

Silver toilet set with box, 1680–90

Made by Anthony Nelme, London, England
Silver
18 cm x 52 cm x 40 cm
43.257–43.265

This late-seventeenth century toilet set, purchased by William Burrell in 1926, was used by his wife Constance, Lady Burrell, as her dressing table silver.

The French ritual of the 'toilette' – the process and preparation of washing and dressing – grew in popularity in British noble households during the second half of the seventeenth century. The 'toilette' took place in a bedroom or dressing room with a toilet service; a set of objects used to dress or store cosmetics, perfumes, accessories, and clothing.

Fashionable toilet services created in silver ranged in size and the number of objects. The mirror was placed centrally on the dressing space, with the other silver objects laid in front.

By the late-eighteenth century it was common for toilet services to be used for travelling, packed into a customized box for storage. This service has a bespoke wooden box with lifting lid, lined in blue velvet, with compartments to hold four smaller silver boxes, silver casket, clothes brush, comb brush, pincushion, and a standing mirror. The individual silver objects are engraved with a 12-pointed *estoile* in a lozenge, for the Hurst family of Lincolnshire; it is highly likely that this service was once owned by a member of this family.

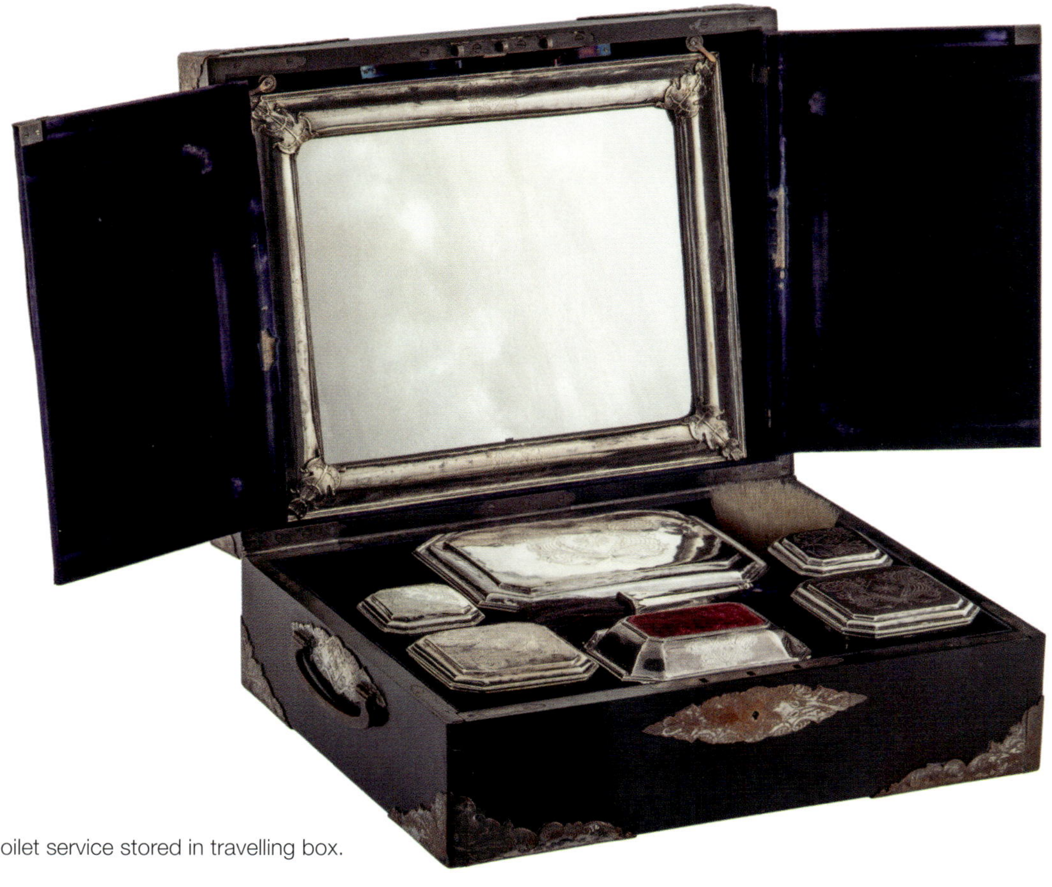

Silver toilet service stored in travelling box.

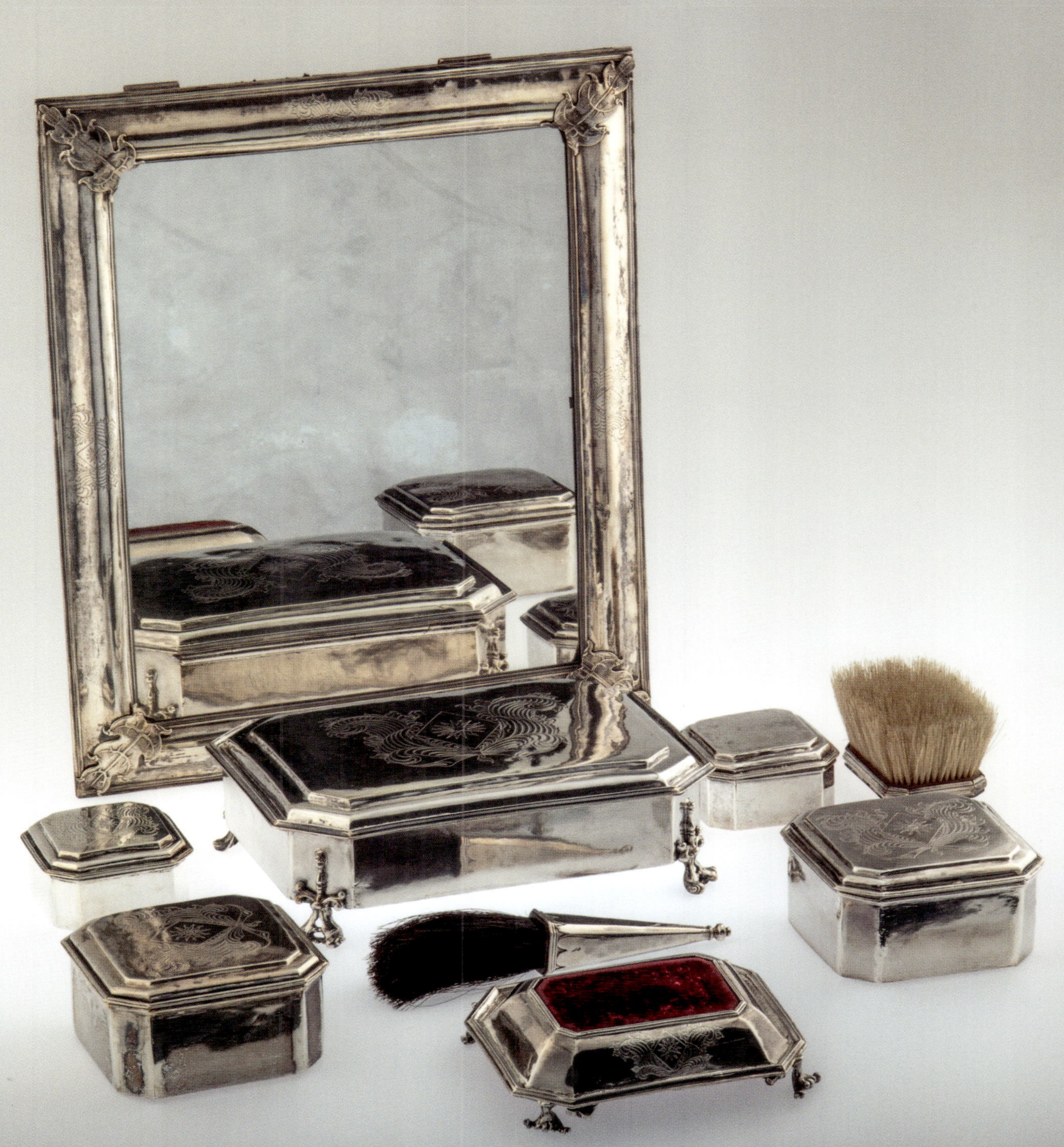

Silver Marks

British silver wares are typically punched with a series of marks to regulate the quality of the silver used and to assure consumers that the silver meets trading standards. Common marks are the town mark, where the silver was tested, the standard mark, a date letter, and a maker's mark.

To independently trade within the City of London, a craftsperson was required to become a member, or freeman, of one of the Livery Companies that supported various trades. The Worshipful Company of Goldsmiths, established in 1327, regulated the silver and gold trade in London.

In 1300, the leopard's head was introduced as the official mark of King Edward I (1239–1307) signifying that silver objects contained the 92.5% silver standard required. This was the standard demanded for coin, which allowed for objects to be melted down into currency. This mark was later known as the town mark for London. In 1478, to deter goldsmiths from striking the leopard's head on substandard silver, which in turn devalued currency, all silver objects had to be checked, or assayed, by officials of the Goldsmiths' Company, at their headquarters, the Goldsmiths' Hall. At this time, the leopard's head was revised to include a crown and a date letter was introduced. The date letter changed annually when the new Assay Master was elected in May. In 1544, the lion passant was introduced as the sterling standard mark, further authenticating the quality of the silver used.

Makers' marks, denoting the silversmith who crafted the piece, were mandatory from 1363. Silversmiths each had a specialist punch personalized with their mark to be struck on the silver they produced. From the late-seventeenth century silversmiths were required to register their unique mark at the Goldsmiths' Hall, made of their initials. At the introduction of the Britannia Standard in 1697 (see p.40) silversmiths registered new marks of the first two letters of their surname.

Makers' marks are also known as 'sponsor marks' as there is no guarantee that the registered individual of the mark actually made the object; it could be the work of a journeyman employed in their workshop or made by another silversmith not yet registered at the Company. However, the workshop owner, was required to present the silver for assay, meaning their mark was stamped on the silver.

Provincial regions of silver trade were established in towns and cities like York, Chester, Exeter, Newcastle and Birmingham. In Scotland, metalworking guilds in Edinburgh and Glasgow regulated the trade of silver wares in these areas. Each city had its own unique town mark (see pp.42 and 43 for examples).

Opposite: Marks found on two-handled cup (43.104), from top clockwise, London date letter for 1723–24, maker's mark 'IC' surmounted by crown and *cinquefoil* for Jonah Clifton, standard mark of lion passant, and leopard's head crowned, town mark for London.

Marrow scoop, 1718–19
Made by John Holland I, London, England
Silver
21.5 cm x 2.4 cm x 1.4 cm
43.201

The increased demand for domestic silverware in
the late-seventeenth century led to the unscrupulous
practice of melting coin for silver wares. To prevent
this, in 1697 a new silver standard was enforced at
95.84%. Known as the Britannia standard, all
silver produced to this higher quality, like this marrow
spoon, was marked with the figure of Britannia,
in place of the lion passant. The leopard's head
crowned was also replaced by a new mark known
as the lion's head erased; it had a ragged edge as
if it had been torn from the body. These new marks
were used until 1720, when the sterling standard of
92.5% was reintroduced, though some silversmiths
after this time still created silver to the higher Britannia
standard.

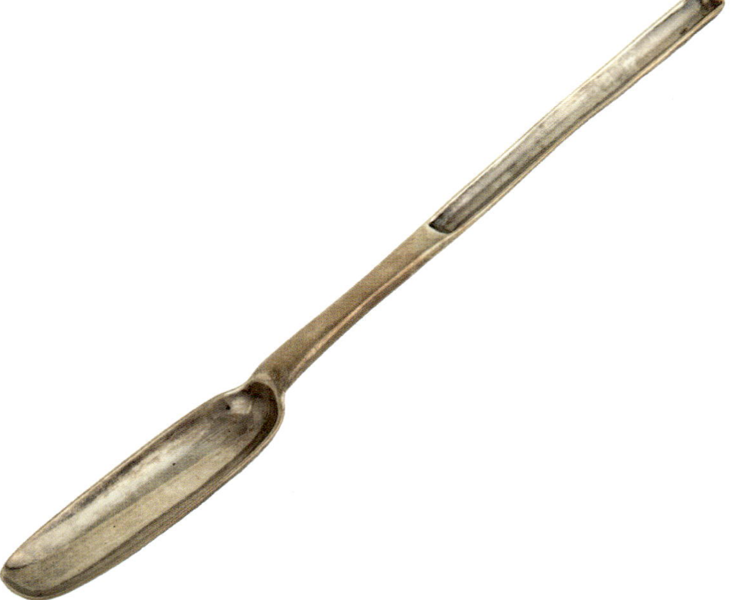

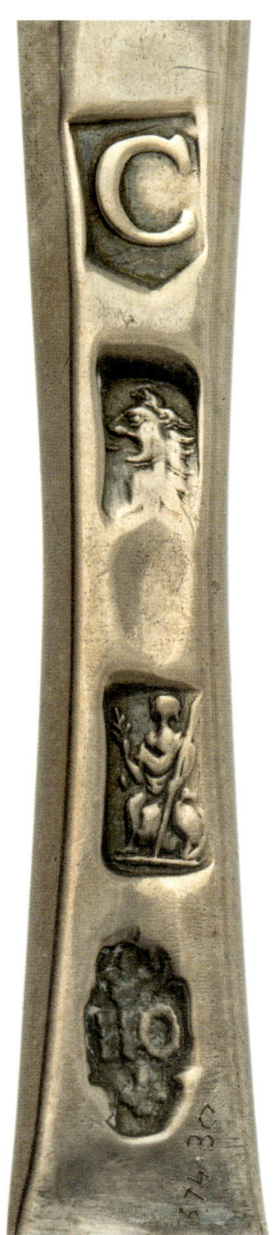

This spoon bears London date letter for 1719–20,
lion's head erased, the Britannia mark, and maker's
mark 'HO' between *fleur-de-lys* for John Holland,
all on the reverse of the stem.

Argyle pot, 1796–97

Made by Henry Chawner and John Emes, London,
England
Silver, wood
15 cm x 20.6 cm x 8.5 cm
43.130

This argyle pot is stamped with an additional
fifth mark of the king's head (George III
(1738–1820)), known as the duty mark. During
the early eighteenth century, silversmiths were
forced to pay additional tax, paying 6d. (pence)
per 1 ounce produced of silver. Although this was
eventually replaced by a flat fee in the mid-eighteenth
century, the duty on silver was reinforced in 1784 to
raise funds for the Crown. Until 1890, silver could
only be assayed for sale once duty was paid, and
marked with the duty mark, usually depicting the
head of the current ruling monarch.

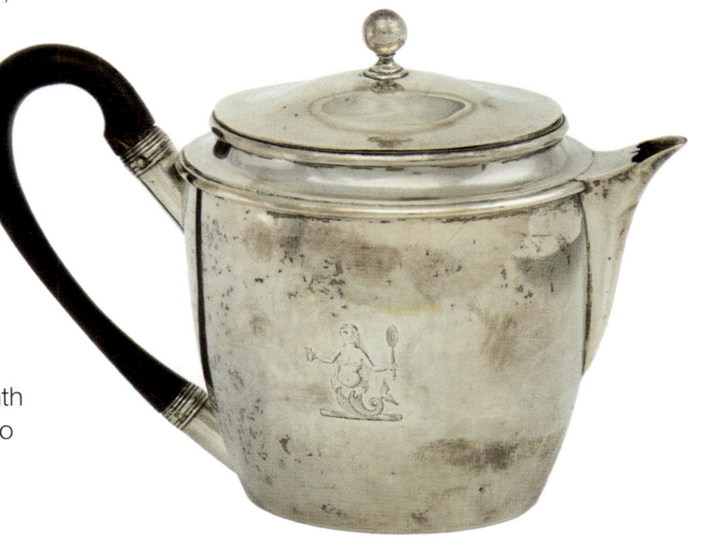

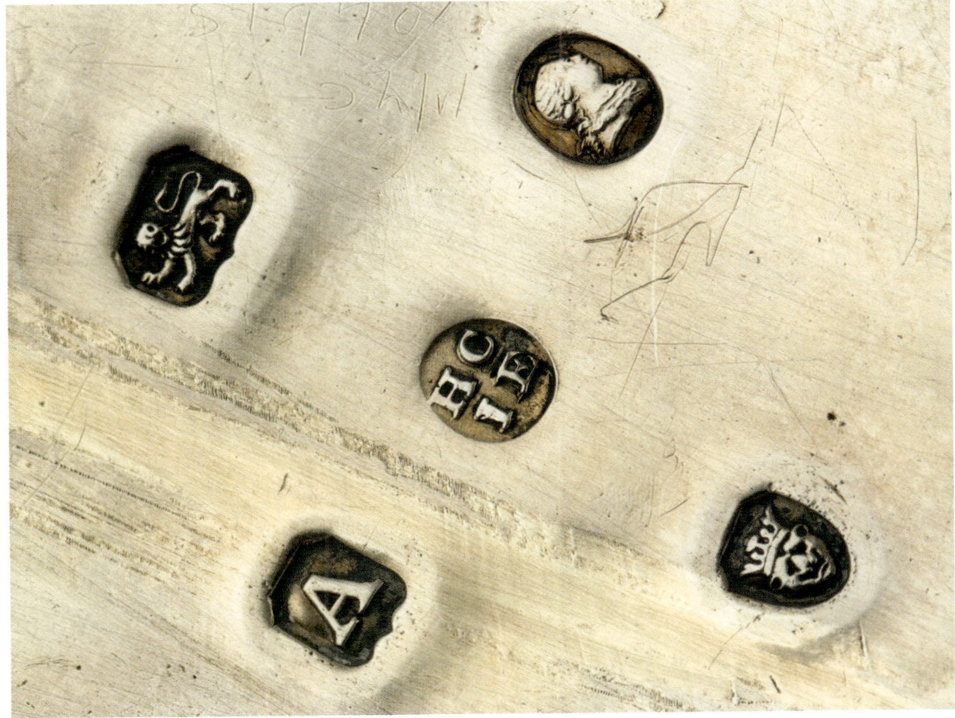

Marks on argyle pot: leopard's
head crowned, lion passant,
king's head duty mark (George III),
London date letter for 1796–97,
and makers' mark 'HC' over 'IE'
for London silversmiths, Henry
Chawner and John Emes.

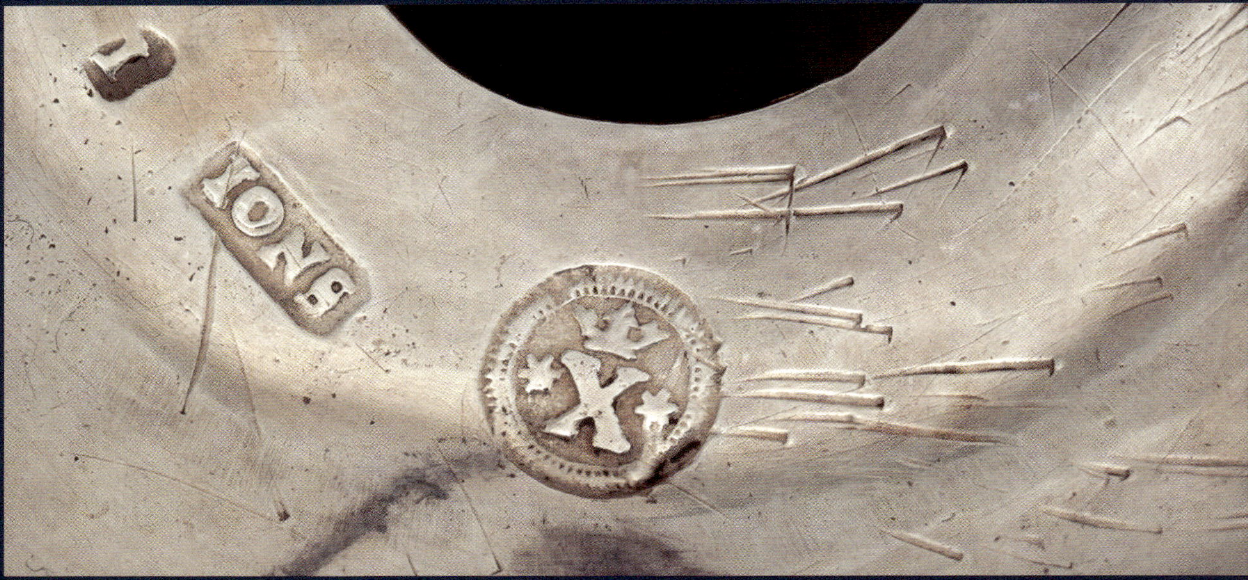

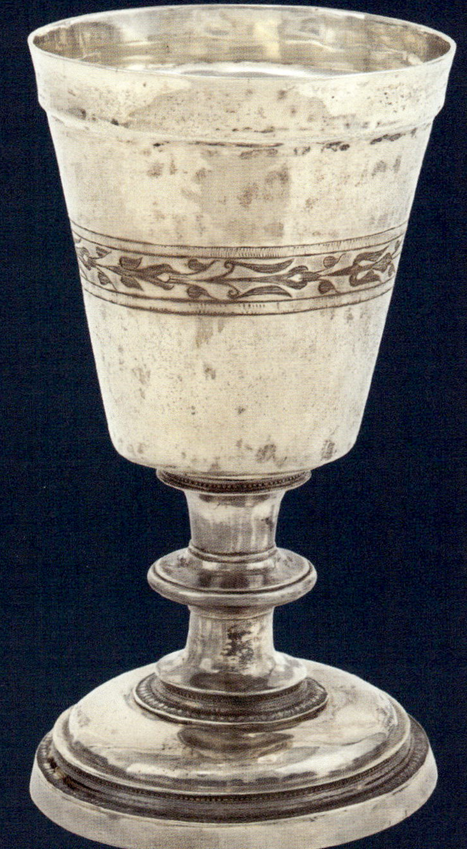

Communion cup with paten cover, 1574

Made by John Jones, Exeter, England
Silver
17.3 cm x 8.7 cm x 8.9 cm
43.10.1-2

This communion cup with cover, dated 1574, bears the town mark of Exeter, an enclosed Roman letter 'X', which is sometimes crowned, circled with a ring of dots. Exeter had an established community of silversmiths working during the sixteenth century, with most makers' marks taking the form of the initial letter of their first name, followed by their surname in a rectangular shield. This cup and cover bears the mark of 'I' 'IONS' for John Jones, one of the most successful Exeter silversmiths of the late sixteenth century. John Jones is known for his religious plate; many examples of communion cups and covers with his mark survive today.

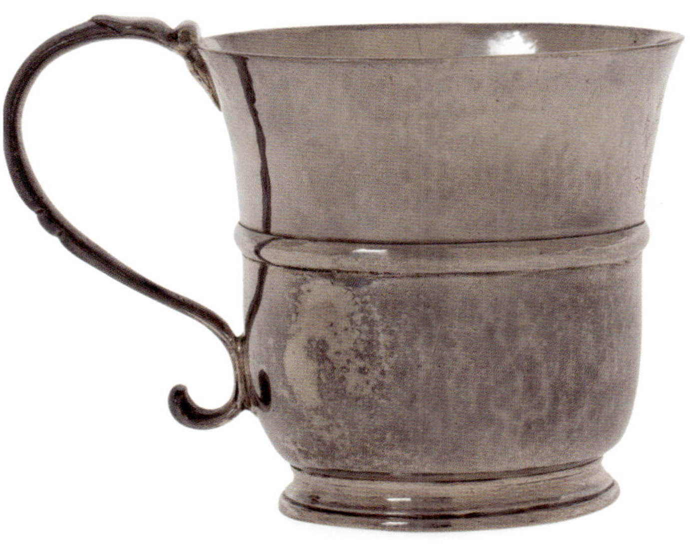

Mug, 1704–05
Made by Colin McKenzie, Edinburgh, Scotland
Assayed by James Penman
Silver
8.9 cm x 11.6 cm x 8.5 cm
43.35

Bell rounded mugs, known as thistle mugs due to their resemblance to the Scottish national flower, were popular in Scotland from the late-seventeenth century. This mug is marked with a castle, the town mark for Edinburgh. From 1681, all Edinburgh silver was checked by an Assay Master, a working goldsmith who was the chief office bearer of the craft within the town. From 1697–1707, James Penman was appointed as Edinburgh Assay Master, testing silver from silversmiths across Edinburgh, marking their work with his conjoined 'JP' mark, as seen on this mug. Along with the Edinburgh date letter for 1704–05, the base of the mug also bears the maker's mark of Edinburgh silversmith Colin McKenzie.

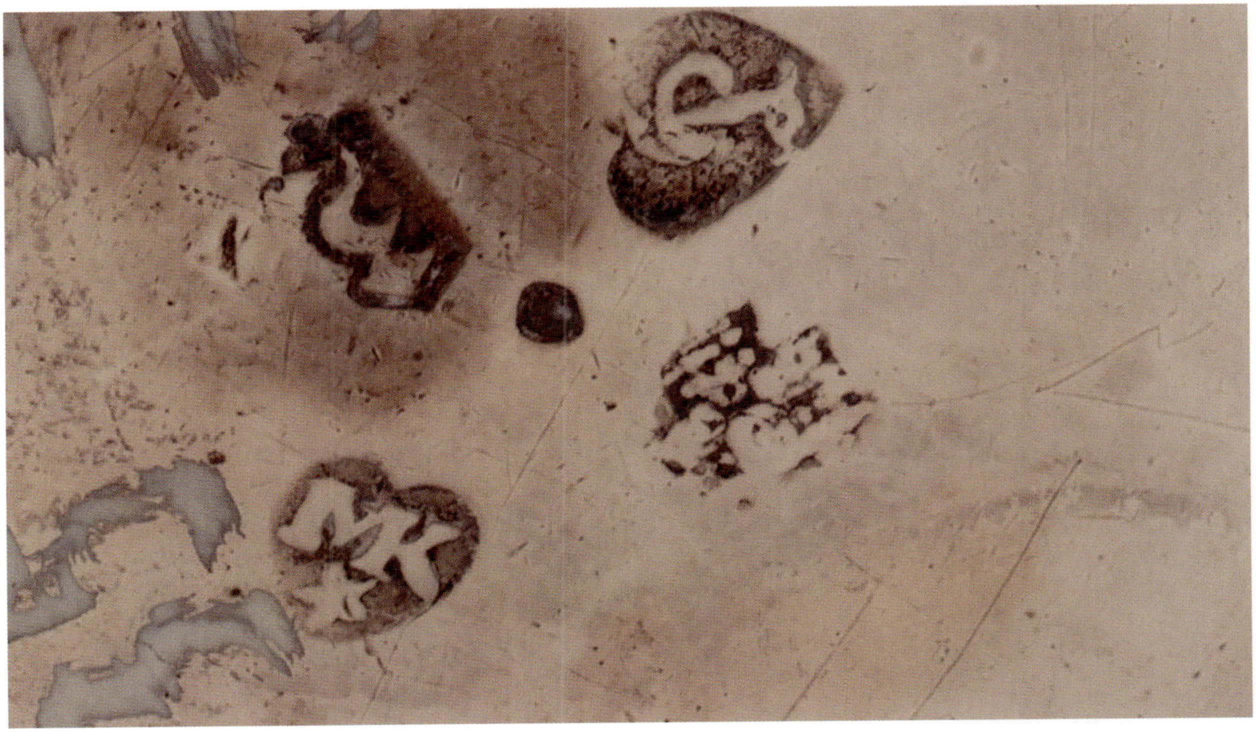

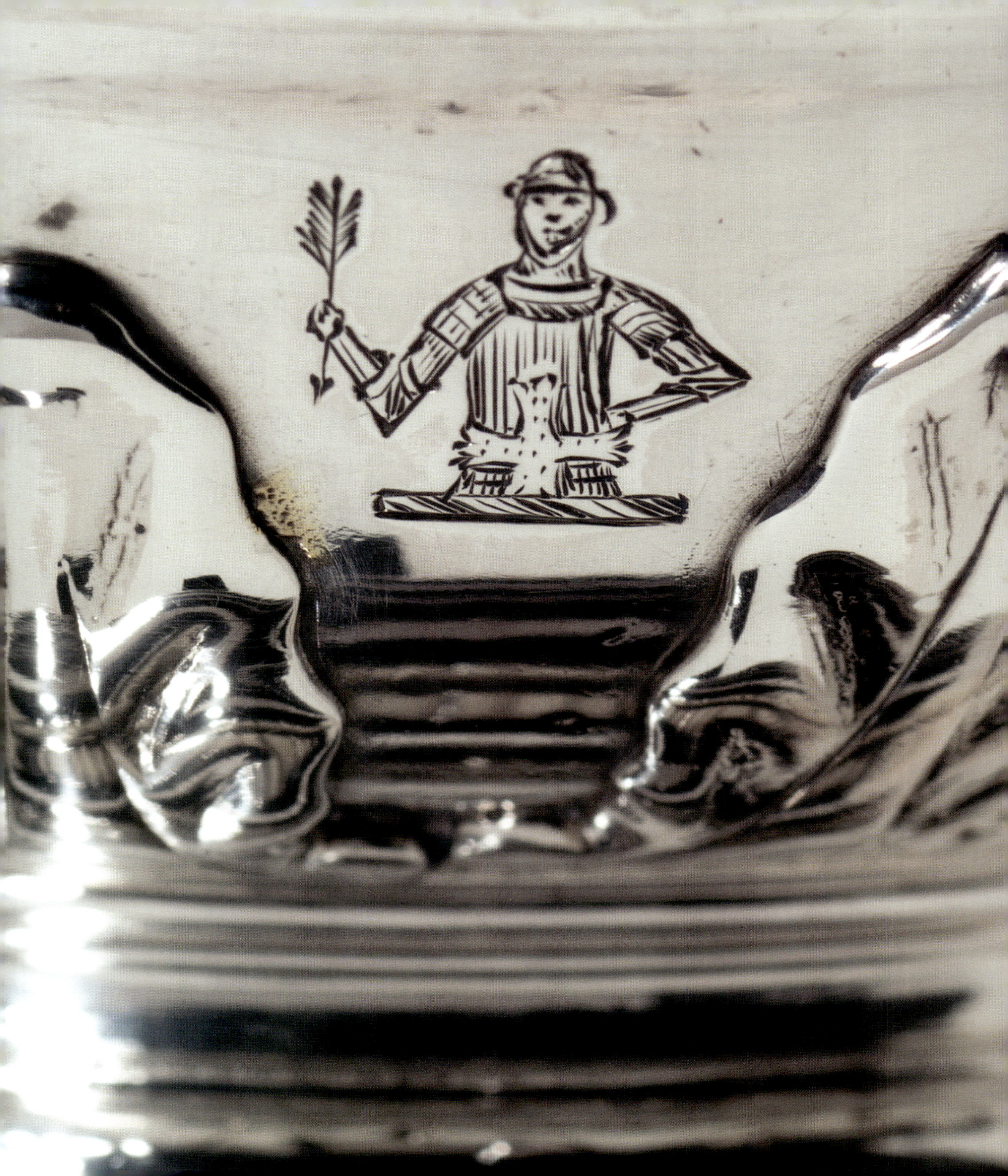

Huguenot Silversmiths

By the end of the seventeenth century, there were several routes available for London silversmiths to gain entry to the Goldsmiths' Company. Silversmiths could be nominated by other freemen of the company or given entry if the prospective member's father was a freeman at the entrant's birth. The most common path was through serving an apprenticeship to a freeman of the Company, for a period of seven years, learning the trade and producing work on behalf of their master.

At the end of the seventeenth century, a large contingent of French Protestant refugees, known as Huguenots, fled their native country of France to England. In 1598 the Edict of Nantes had been proclaimed in France, allowing Protestants the right to worship freely and hold positions of power within the majority Catholic nation. Almost a century later, in 1685 the French King Louis XIV (1638–1715) revoked the Edict of Nantes, leading to the suppression and persecution of Protestants. Seeking religious freedom and security, thousands of Huguenots escaped France and settled in London, where their faith was tolerated. Many refugees were talented craftsmen, experts in textile weaving, ceramics, and silver work.

Some Huguenot families had moved to London before the Revocation; in 1681 Charles II (1630–85) ordered that Huguenots could apply for denization, making them a citizen. Huguenot silversmiths quickly set to work establishing workshops and clientele, working longer hours and at lower, more competitive rates than established London silversmiths. Huguenot metalworkers also brought with them knowledge and skills in the modelling, casting, and engraving of silver in fashionable French styles and designs, which were highly desired by the British elite.

Despite denization status, many Huguenots were prevented from joining the Goldsmiths' Company and having their work assayed at the Goldsmiths' Hall. From 1697 to 1716, a series of petitions against the Huguenot silversmiths was brought before the Goldsmiths' Hall by London silversmiths, anxious over the growing competition from these new craftsmen. Although the majority were unsuccessful, the petitions tried to enforce restrictions, extend time periods Huguenots worked as apprentices, and deny them entry to the Goldsmiths' Company. However, popular demand for Huguenot designs led to many London silversmiths adapting their styles and employing Huguenots within their workshops. A 1711 petition marked the growing need for Huguenot workers, naming them as 'necessitous strangers'. By the 1720s, the Goldsmiths' Hall was required to mark plate of freeman and non-members, lifting restrictions faced by Huguenot silversmiths and allowing them to become radical tastemakers of English silver.

Opposite: Cut-card foliage decoration on silver salt, marked for Huguenot silversmith Anne Tanqueray, 1726–27 (detail; see also pp.48–49). This cut-card foliage design was a common Huguenot decorative motif.

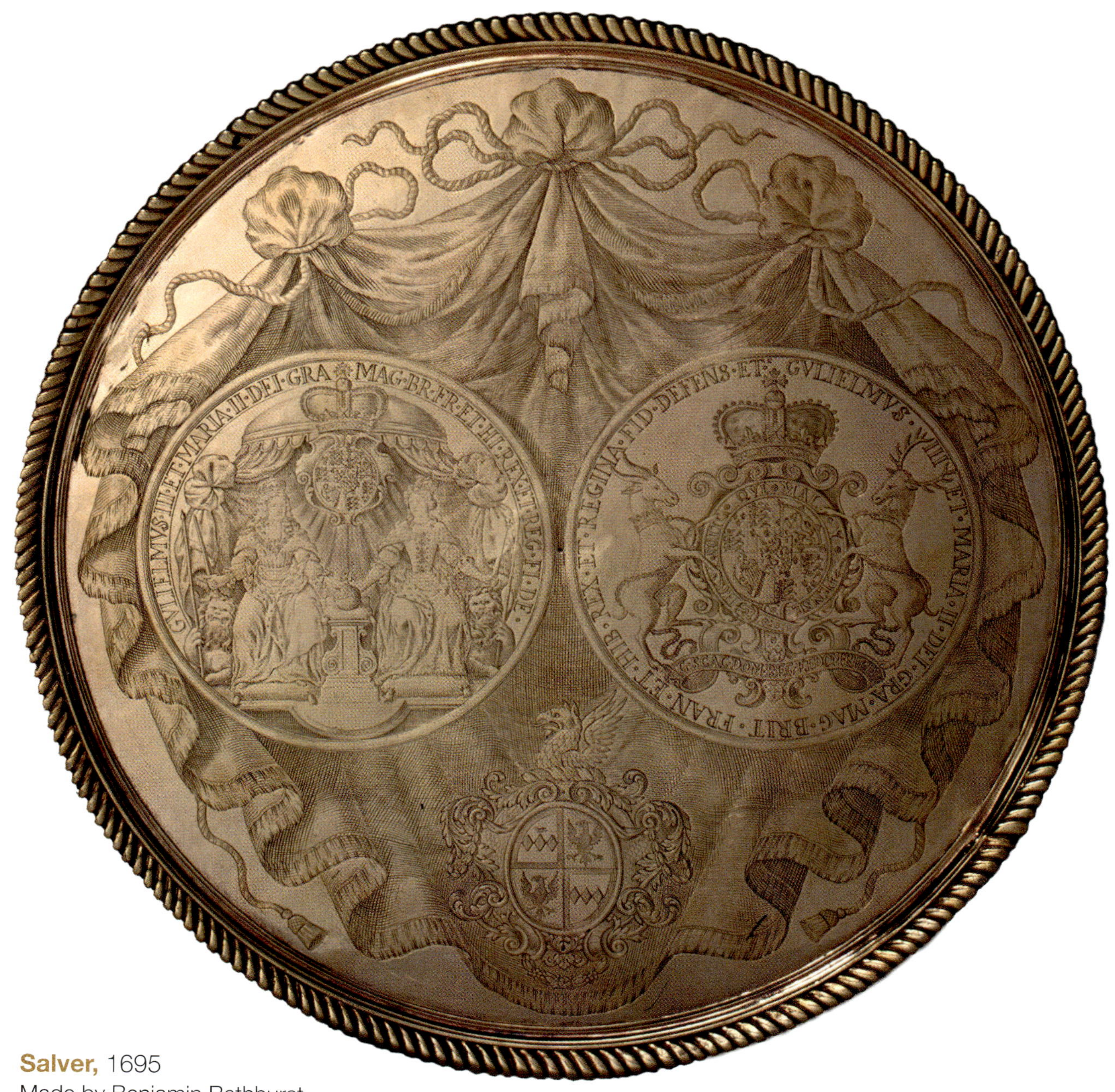

Salver, 1695
Made by Benjamin Bathhurst,
engraved by Simon Gribelin, London, England
Silver-gilt
9 cm x 34.3 cm x 34.3 cm
43.72

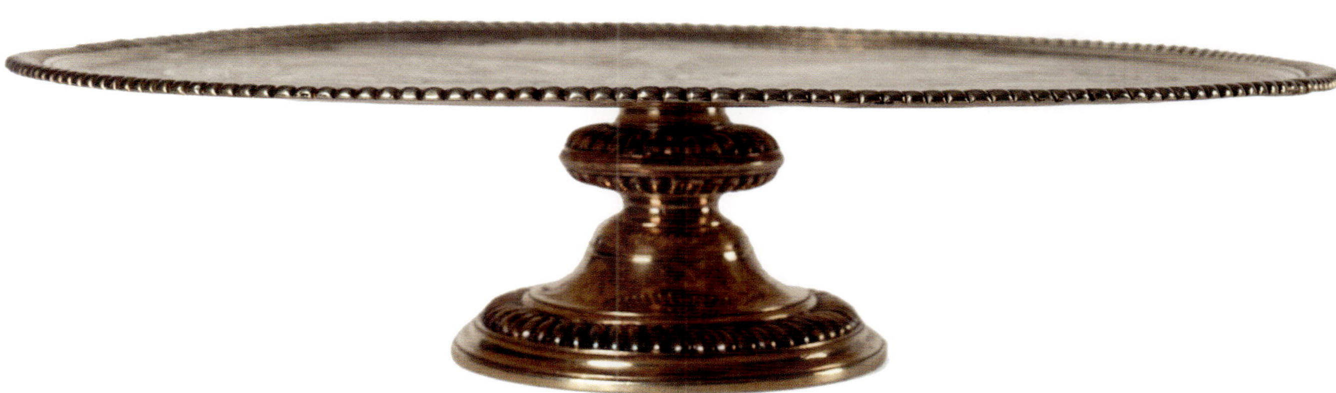

This salver was commissioned by Charles Montagu, 1st Earl of Halifax (1661–1715) to commemorate his role as Chancellor of the Exchequer, to which he was appointed on 10 May 1694. On the death of Queen Mary II (1662–94) in December 1694, the silver seal of the Exchequer with her coat of arms became obsolete. Montagu was allowed to retain the seal, melting it down to create this salver. The salver tray is engraved with dramatic drapery mantling surrounding the front and back of the Exchequer seal; on one side Queen Mary II, and her husband, King William III (1650–1702), enthroned under a canopy; the other side with the Royal coat of arms.

The engraving of this salver was created by Simon Gribelin, a French Huguenot engraver active in London from the 1680s. After leaving France, Gribelin became a member of the Watchmakers' Company, designing and engraving watches. In the late seventeenth century he gained notable commissions engraving salvers of great seals. An album of his designs, *Livre d'Estampes de Sim. Grebelin, fait Relié a Londre*, published in 1722, contains proofs and prints of engraved ornaments that Gribelin created, including the designs for this salver.

The salver, supported by a central gadrooned foot, is marked for silversmith Benjamin Bathurst. The salver tray most likely was crafted and assayed first before being passed on to Gribelin for engraving.

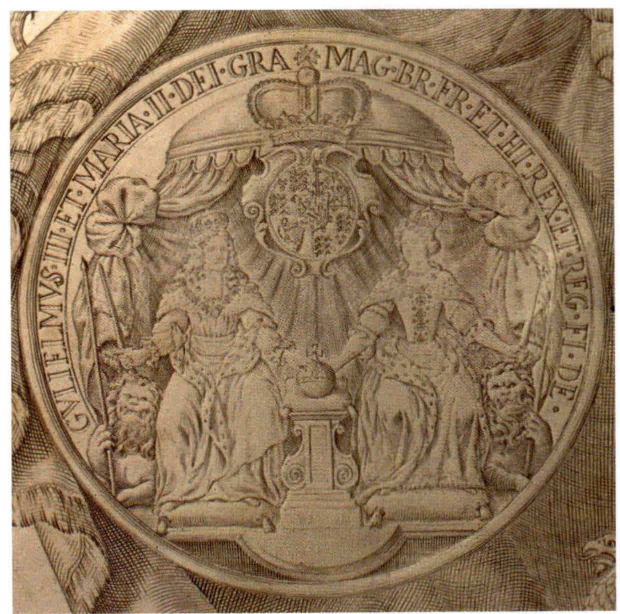

Detail of salver engraving, showing King William III and Queen Mary II.

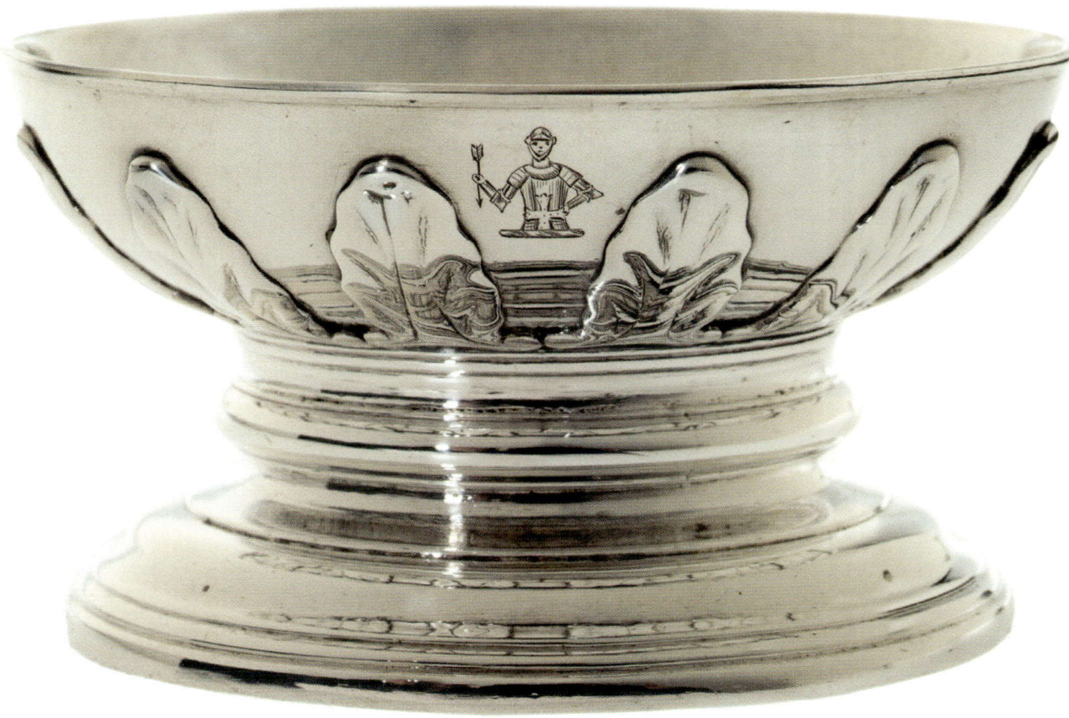

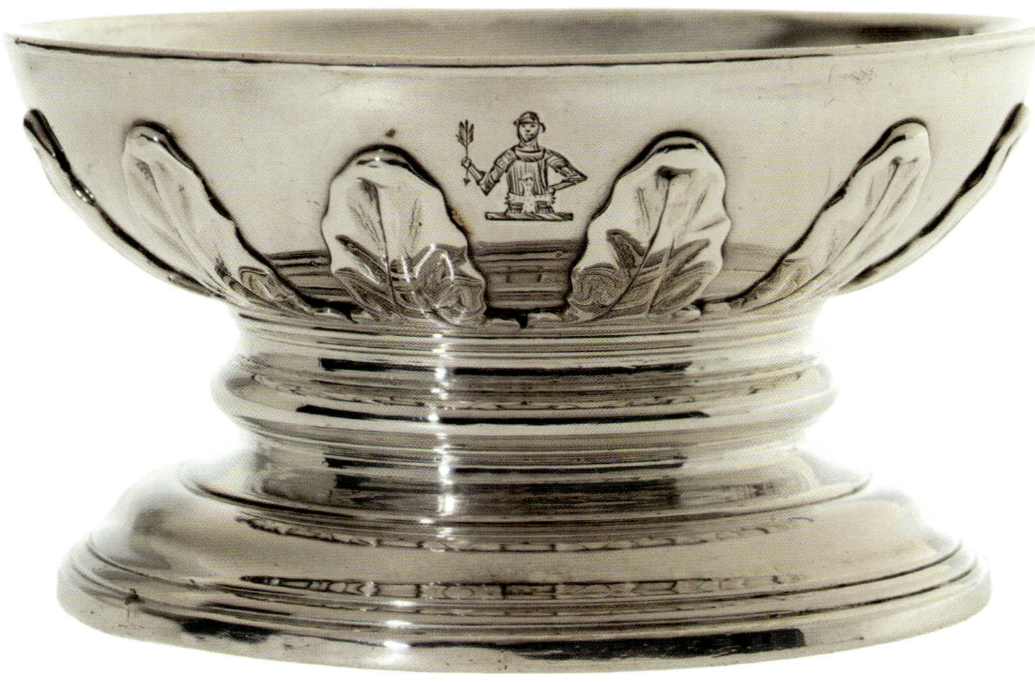

Pairs of salts, 1726–27

Made by Anne Tanqueray, London, England
Silver
48 mm x 89 mm x 89 mm
49 mm x 89 mm x 89 mm
43.148, 43.149

These salts are stamped with the mark of silversmith
Anne Tanqueray (1691–1733), the eldest daughter
of Huguenot goldsmith and banker, David Willaume
(1658–1741). Willaume had fled France before the
1685 Revocation of the Edict of Nantes, establishing
himself as a distinguished goldsmith in London.
Anne married Willaume's apprentice David Tanqueray
in 1717, and most probably produced items of silver
in her husband's workshop. After David Tanqueray's
death in 1724, Anne took over management of the
workshop, registering her own mark into the
Goldsmiths' Company's records; her husband's
original mark, registered in 1713, was scored out
with Anne's name and mark written above. It was
common for widows of silversmiths to take on the
family workshop after the death of their husband,
giving them a unique position in society as both
metalworkers and business owners. The workshop
under Anne's leadership continued to have an
established and successful reputation, with Anne
Tanqueray becoming Subordinate Goldsmith to the
King in 1729, providing silver plate to the royal court
of King George II (1683–1760). At her death in 1733,
Anne Tanqueray left her 'working tools' and 'patterns'
to the care of her executors to be given to her
children, David and Thomas, when they came of age.

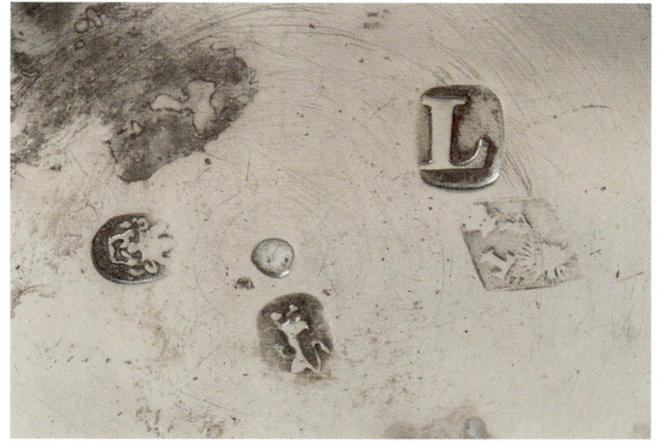

The salts bear Anne Tanqueray's mark: 'AT' between a sun
burst and escallop within a lozenge. In heraldry, widows could
display their coat of arms inside a lozenge. It was common for
female silversmiths' marks to be lozenge-shaped, marking their
widowhood.

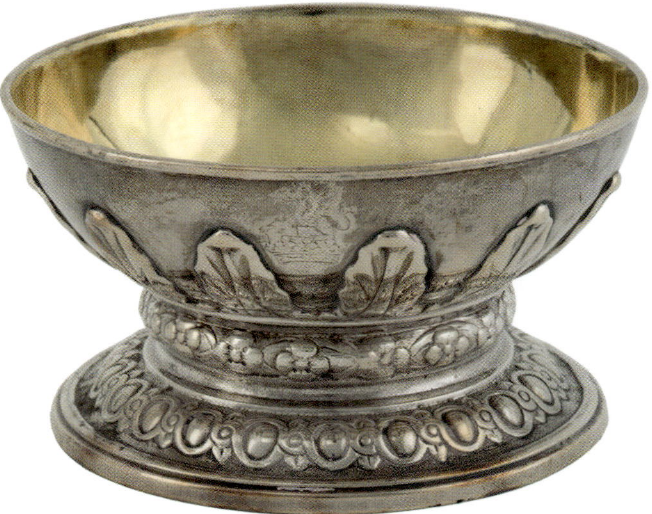

A salt of similar design, dated 1727–28, marked for Tanqueray's
father, David Willaume, was purchased by Sir William Burrell in
1935. (43.146)

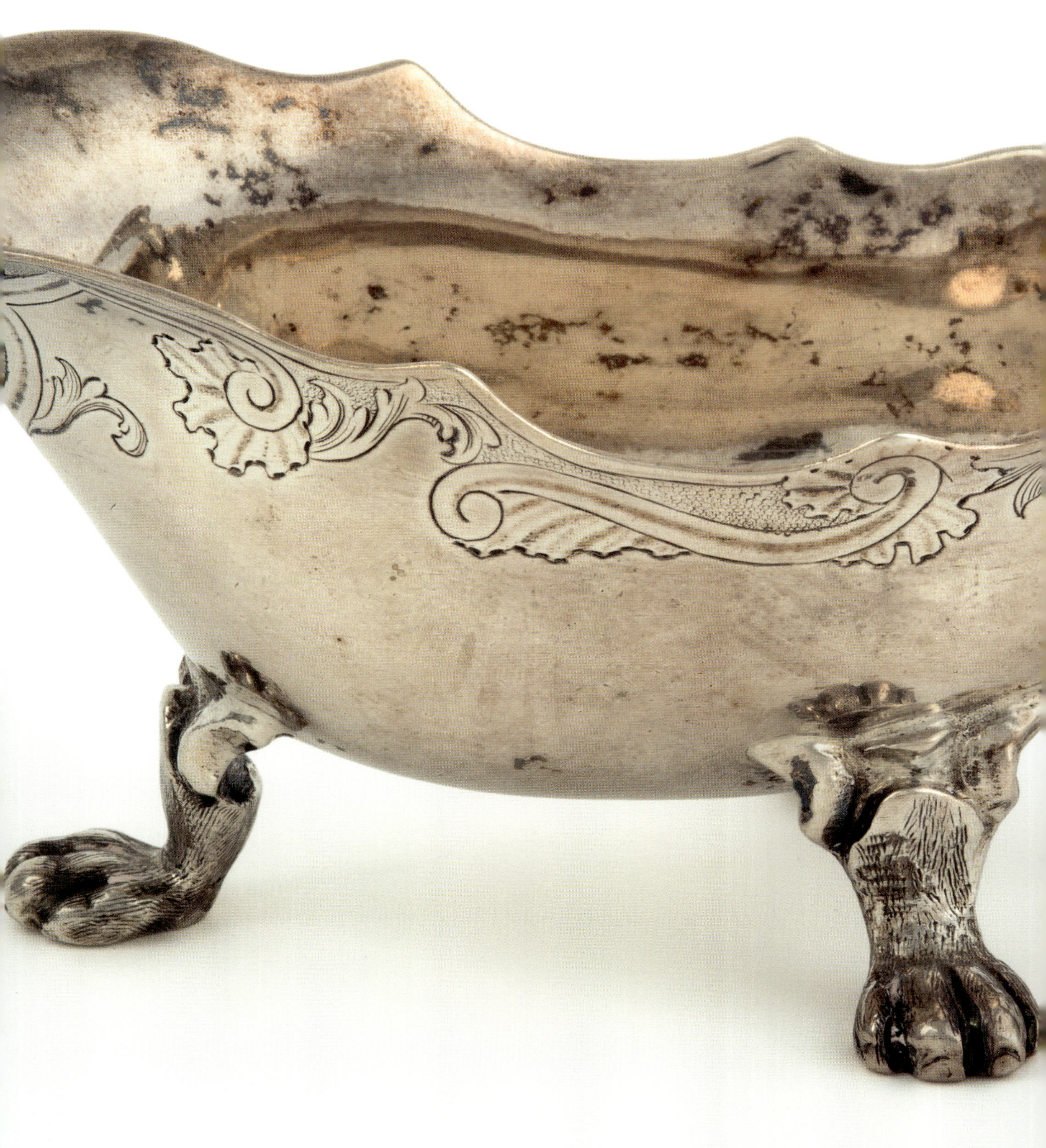

Silver Service

The eighteenth century saw demand for new styles of domestic silverware, influenced by changing tastes of drinking and dining. The consumption of tea, coffee, and hot chocolate became a fashionable pastime across society, with elaborate silver services created for the preparation of the hot beverages, including teapots, cannisters, spoons and bowls. Sugar, used to sweeten tea and prepare magnificent dessert courses, was imported from British plantations in the Americas and Caribbean where enslaved Africans were forced to work in inhumane conditions to produce sugar. Silver for sugar, including casters and bowls, reflect the widespread use of this commodity and show the integral influence of the transatlantic slave trade in the development of silverware held to store the goods produced by this triangular trade.

Dining fashions also changed with the adoption of French styles, known as *à la française*. Prepared dishes of food were laid on the table for guests to help themselves and serve each other throughout the courses. For the wealthy, silver played a vital role in dressing the table, with candlesticks, cutlery, dishes, sauceboats, and salvers used alongside other luxury materials such as porcelain and glass.

It is difficult to discern how much of the silver collected by the Burrells was used by them for their own dining. From surviving correspondence, William Burrell describes a 'silver room' within the family home of Hutton Castle, most likely a lockable room to store household silver. The Purchase Books, in which Burrell recorded all his purchases from 1911 until his death in 1958, give glimpses into which silver objects were used by the family. In the 1951 Purchase Book, silver objects are listed as 'gifted' from William and Constance Burrell, including objects previously recorded in the purchase records; Constance Burrell's eighteenth-century silver toilet service (see also p.36–37), purchased in 1929, was added to the collection on 20 April 1951. A list of 17 silver objects, including, salts, plates, teapots, and cream jugs were gifted from the Burrells on 26 April 1951 with explicit instructions from William Burrell that they are 'to remain at Hutton Castle until the deaths of my wife and myself'. These items (see also p.68, 70–71) were most likely in use by the Burrells as personal dining ware, until Constance's death in 1961.

Opposite: Sauceboat supported by lion feet, dated 1736–37, purchased by Sir William Burrell in 1928 (detail, see also p.62–63).

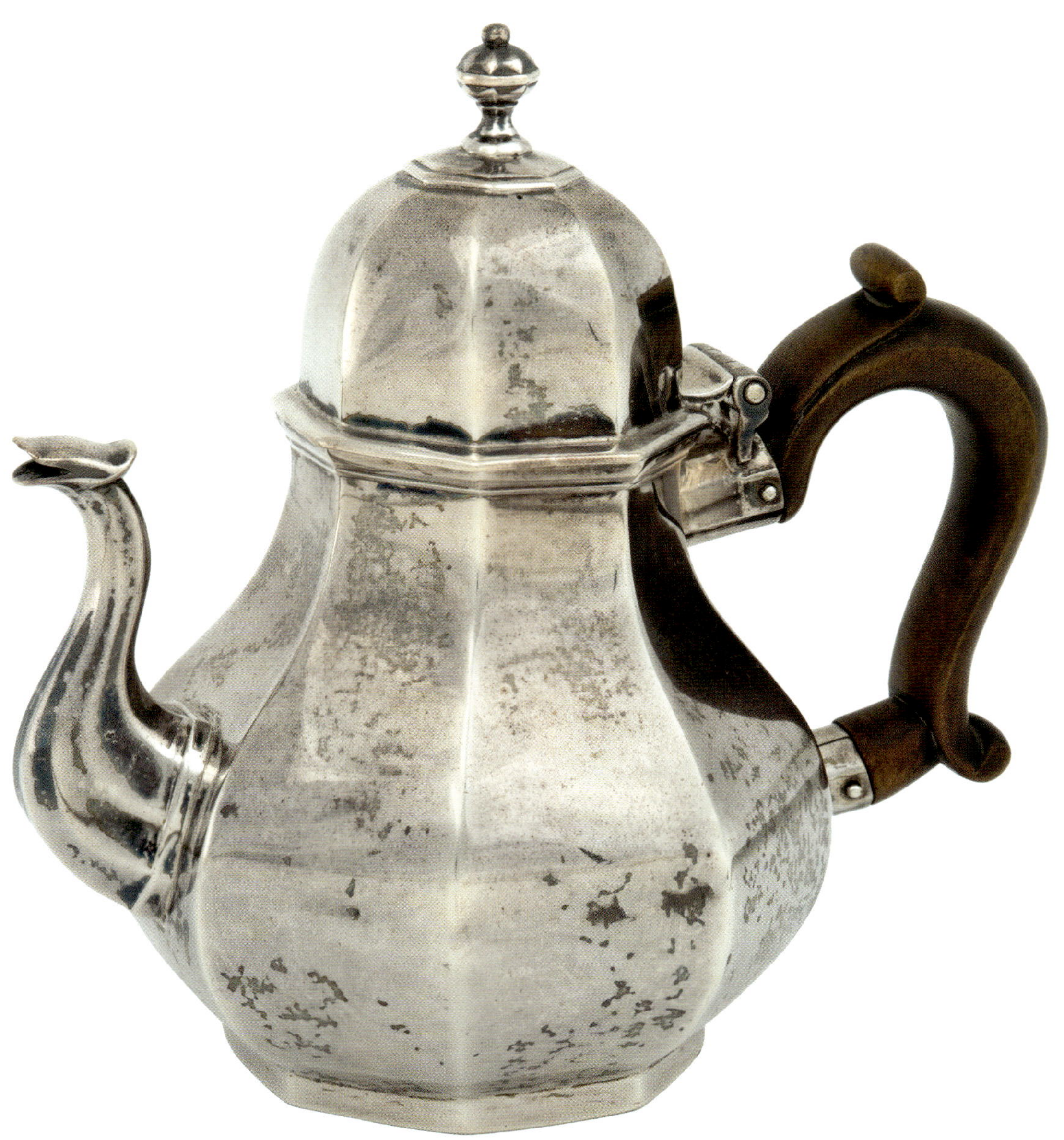

Teapot, 1716–17
Made by Joseph Bell I, London, England
Silver
17.1 cm x 17.5 cm x 11 cm
43.126

This silver teapot has a pear-shaped octagonal facetted body on a short straight foot, hinged dome cover with knop, and serpentine spout. Late seventeenth-century teapots of tall conical form eventually fell out of fashion, with rounded teapots, like this example, becoming popular from the start of the eighteenth century. Tea, unlike food, could be offered at any time, served during social visits with the woman of the household able to prepare tea for guests without assistance from household servants. This teapot has a scrolling wooden handle; the wood stayed cool, protecting the pourer's hands from the silver body, which was hot from the boiling liquid inside.

Tea cannister, 1707–08
Made by Thomas Ash, London, England
Silver
15.8 cm x 11.6 cm x 8.3 cm
43.142

This tea cannister stored dried tea leaves needed for
the preparation of tea. The leaves were poured from
the small neck, the domed cap used for measuring
the desired amount. The front is engraved with the
letter 'G' identifying its use for green tea. Cannisters
were often made in pairs, one for green tea, and the
other for black tea; it was customary to have
both varieties on offer at tea services. Both
teas were imported from China by the East
India Trading Company, the black tea so
named because of its darker leaf. It is
possible this cannister once had a
partner inscribed with 'B' for black tea.

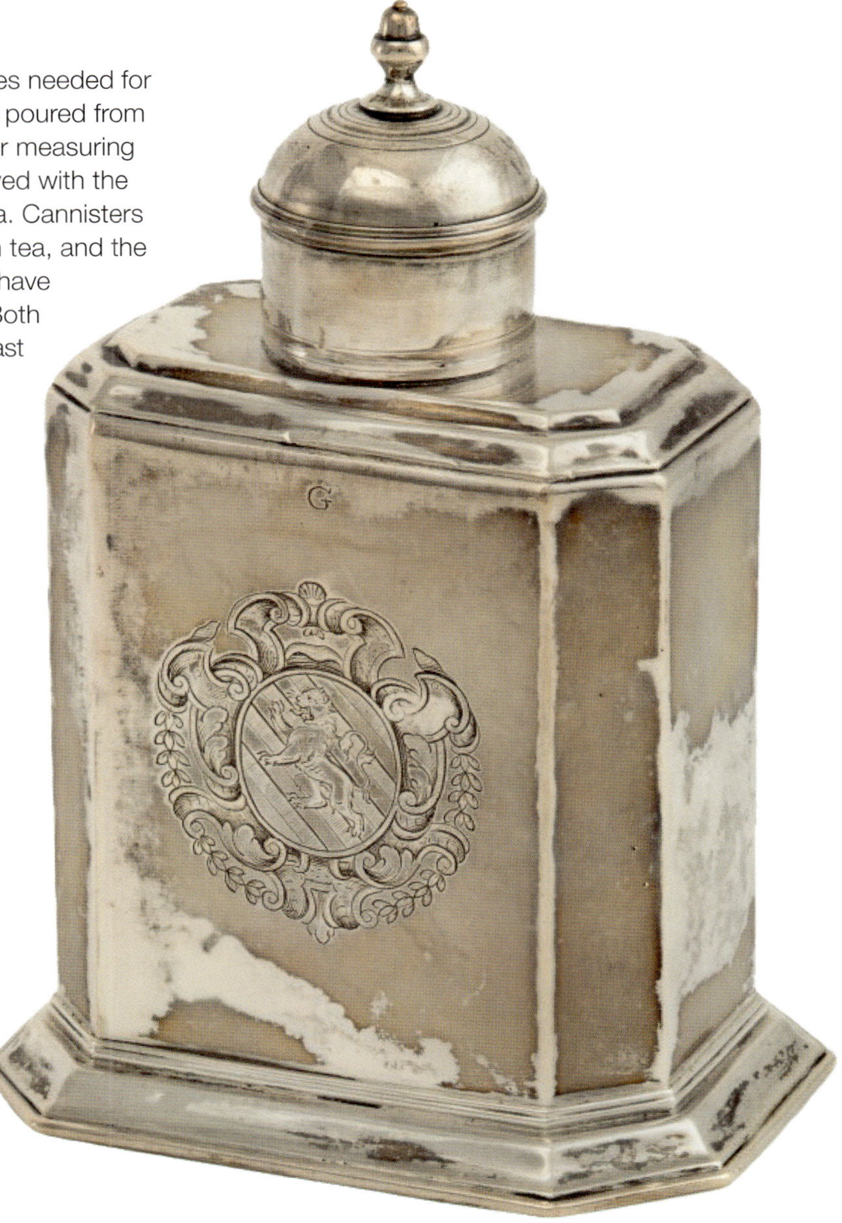

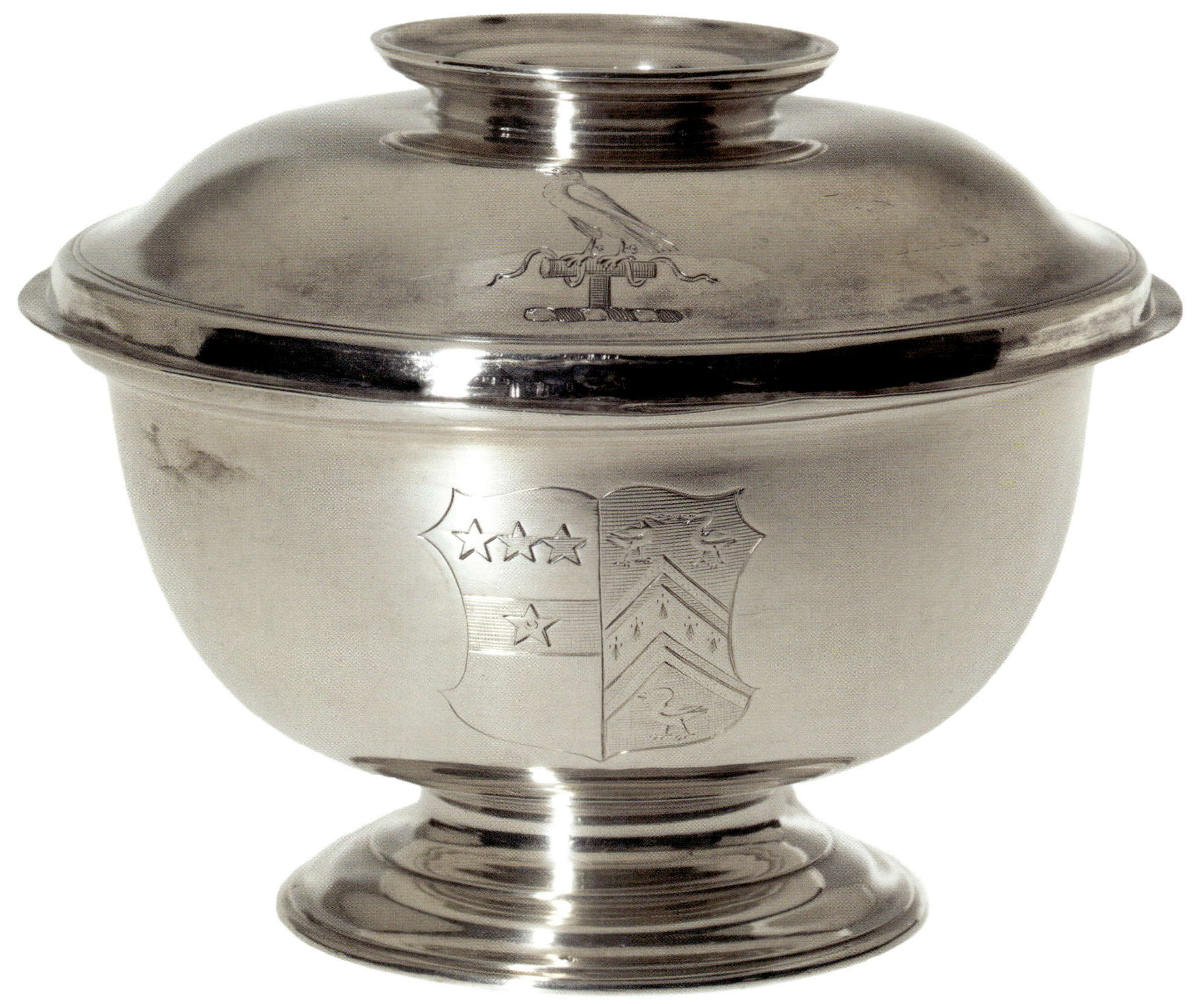

Sugar bowl with cover, 1729–30
Made by Elizabeth Goodwin, London, England
Silver
9 cm x 11.5 cm x 11.5 cm
43.20

This sugar bowl was probably once part of a larger tea service owned by a member of the Towneley family of Royle, Lancashire; the bowl is engraved with their family crest and armorial. The bowl held sugar scrapings, chipped from a large sugar cone. The cover of this bowl could be inverted, creating a saucer for placing serving spoons or sugar tongs. The bowl bears the mark of Elizabeth Goodwin, who registered her mark at the Goldsmiths' Hall in 1729, on the death of her silversmith husband, James Goodwin.

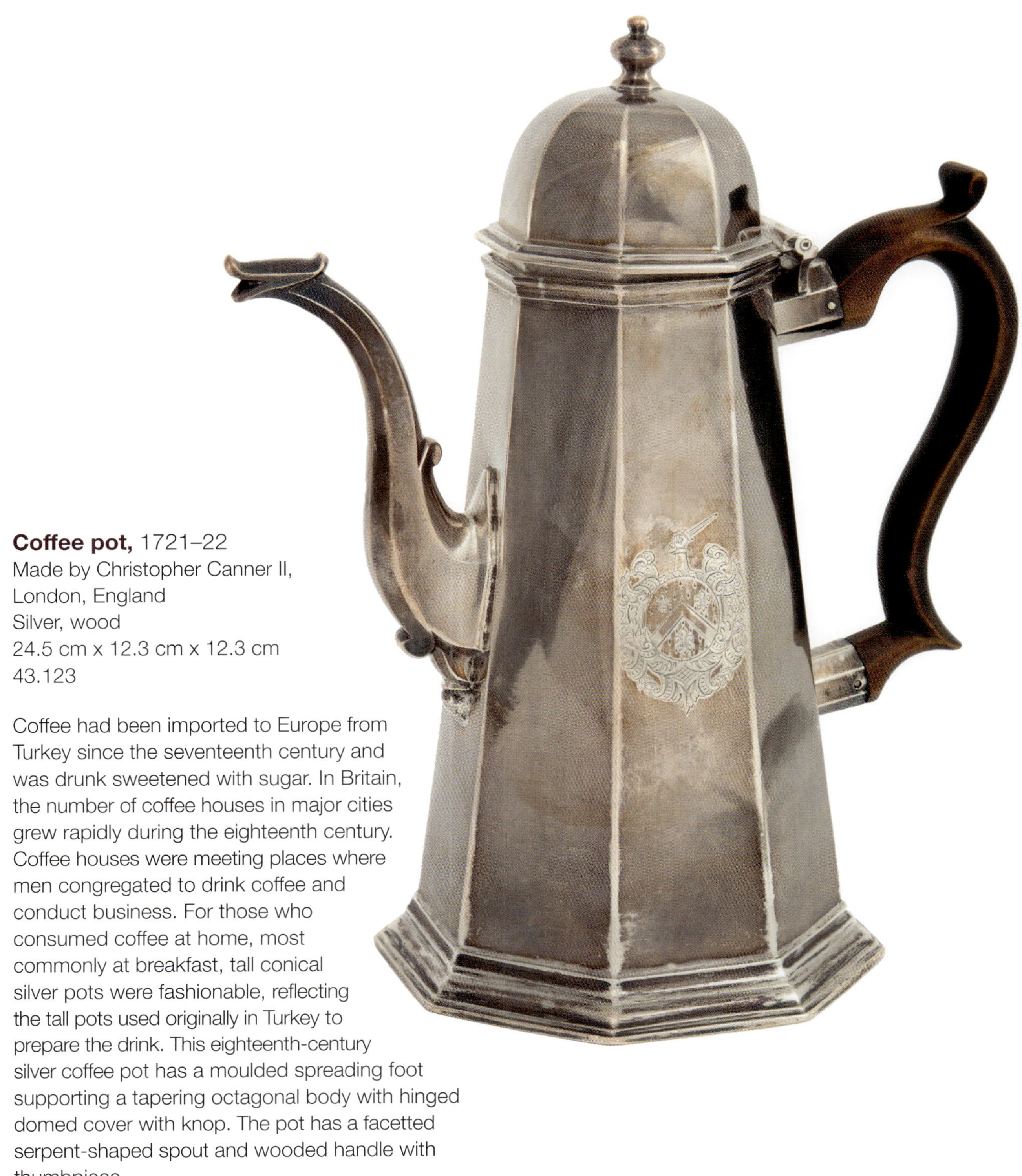

Coffee pot, 1721–22
Made by Christopher Canner II,
London, England
Silver, wood
24.5 cm x 12.3 cm x 12.3 cm
43.123

Coffee had been imported to Europe from
Turkey since the seventeenth century and
was drunk sweetened with sugar. In Britain,
the number of coffee houses in major cities
grew rapidly during the eighteenth century.
Coffee houses were meeting places where
men congregated to drink coffee and
conduct business. For those who
consumed coffee at home, most
commonly at breakfast, tall conical
silver pots were fashionable, reflecting
the tall pots used originally in Turkey to
prepare the drink. This eighteenth-century
silver coffee pot has a moulded spreading foot
supporting a tapering octagonal body with hinged
domed cover with knop. The pot has a facetted
serpent-shaped spout and wooded handle with
thumbpiece.

Object in Focus

Chocolate pot, 1702–03
Made by William Lukin, London, England
Silver
23.6 cm x 15.4 cm x 13.2 cm
43.121

Along with tea and coffee, drinking hot chocolate was popular during the late-seventeenth and early-eighteenth centuries. Chocolate is derived from cocoa beans, which were initially imported to Europe in the seventeenth century from South America. To create the chocolate required for drinking, the cocoa beans were ground, crushed, and flattened into chocolate discs. The chocolate was then crumbled and mixed with hot water and spices to make the beverage; some recipes made hot chocolate with alcohol, typically wine or port.

Early silver chocolate pots are often formed with a handle set at a right angle to the spout. However, these types of handles are also found on coffee pots of the period. The distinguishing feature of a chocolate pot is a detachable finial, or with this example, a hinged finial, creating a small opening at the top of the lid. The prepared hot chocolate drink was thick in consistency, requiring the liquid to be whisked to make it light for sipping. A stirring stick, known as a 'molinet', would be inserted into this gap to froth the chocolate inside, without the need to remove the domed lid and risk the beverage inside becoming cold.

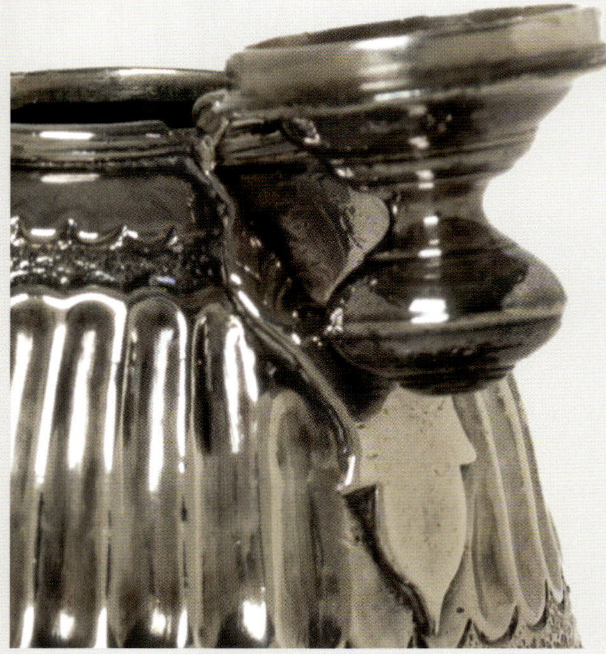

Hinged finial for the insertion of stirring stick to whisk the hot chocolate (detail; 43.121).

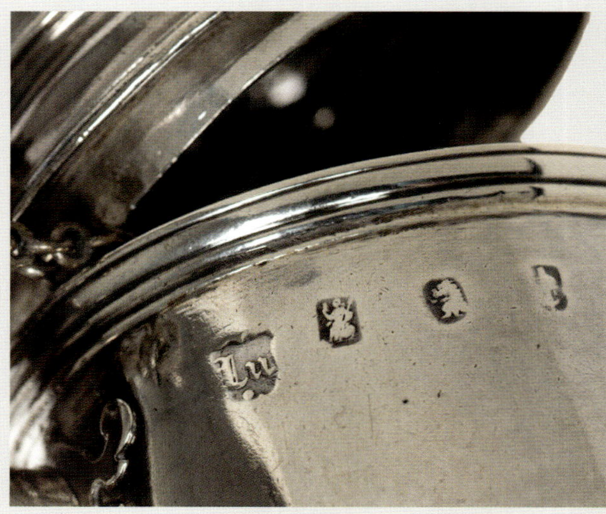

Marks: Britannia; lion's head erased, blurred London date letter, probably 1702–03; maker's mark 'Lu' over pellet for William Lukin.

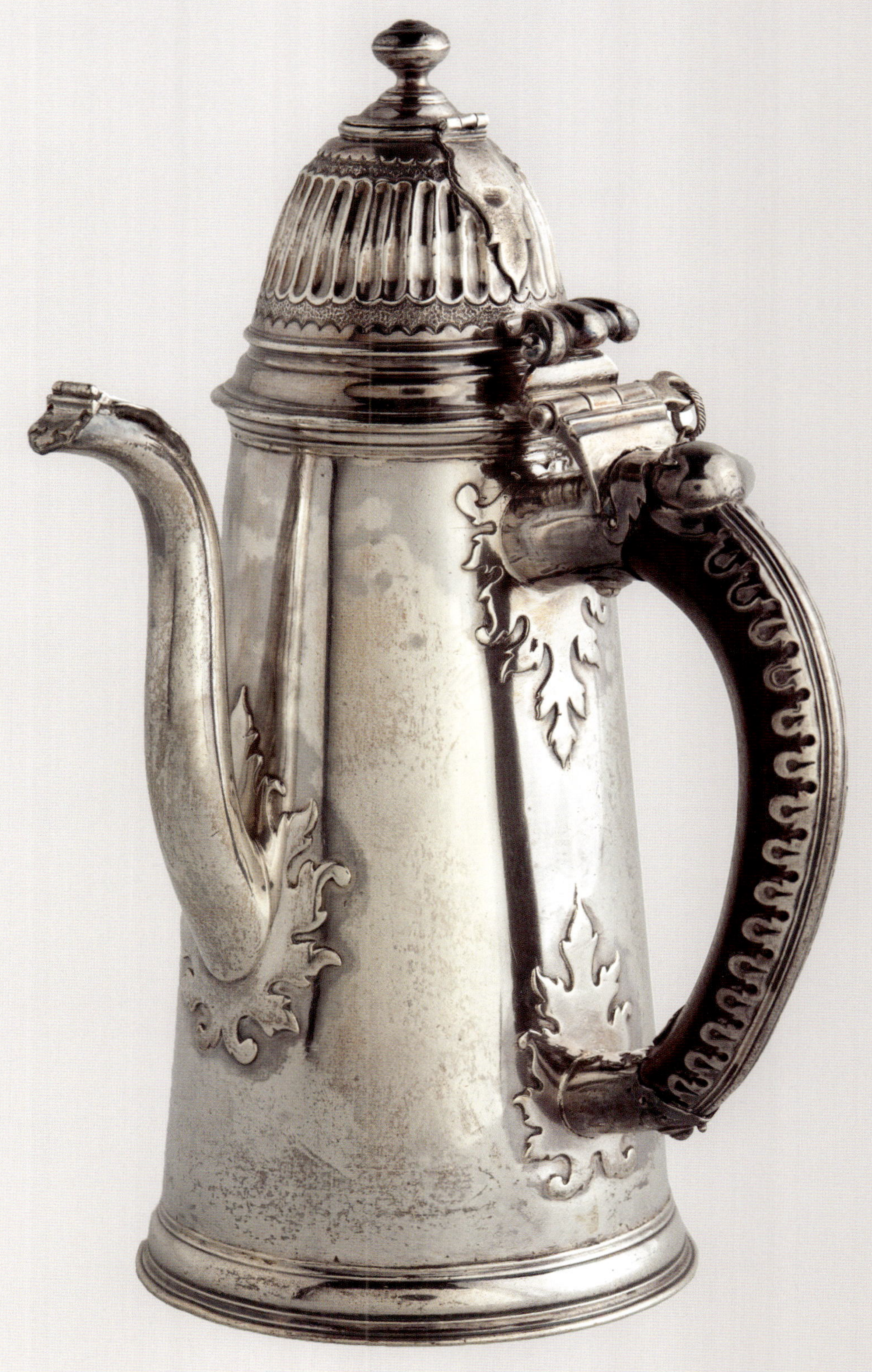

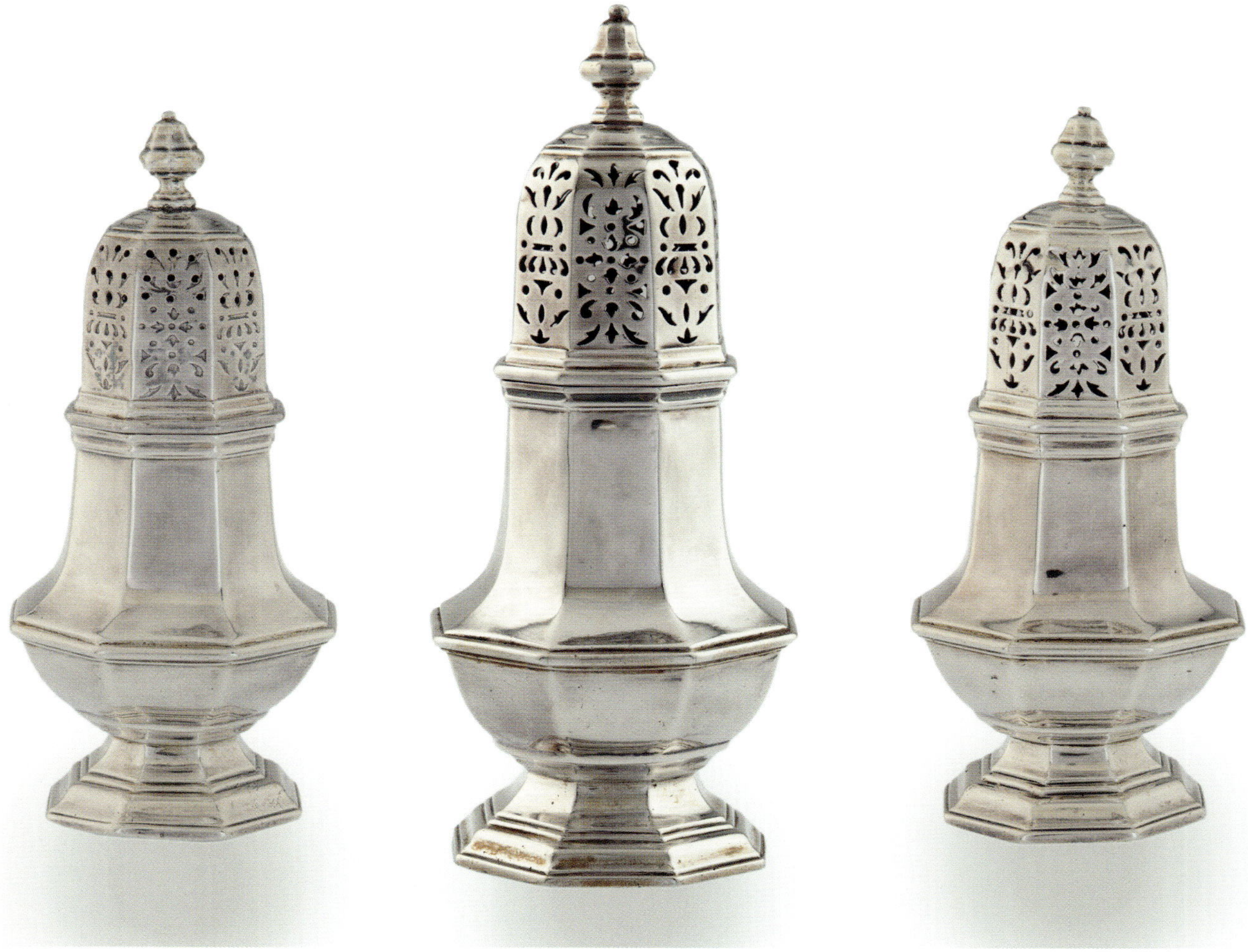

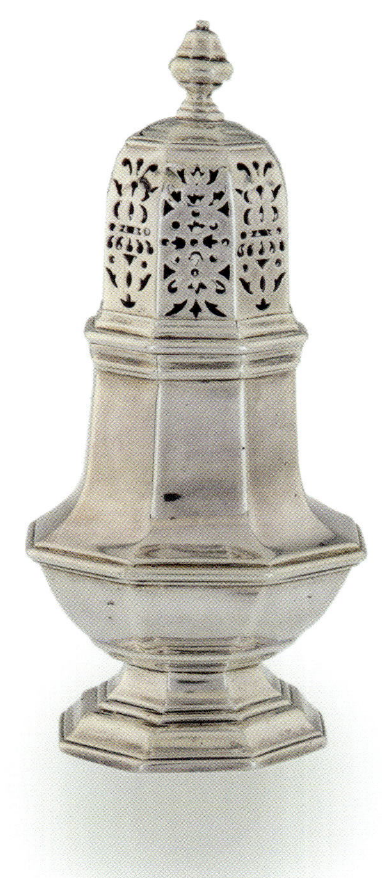

Sugar and spice casters, 1723–24
Made by James Mitchellsone, Edinburgh, Scotland
Silver
15.3 cm x 7.1 cm x 7.2 cm
18.4 mm x 8 cm x 8 cm
15.3 cm x 7 cm x 7 cm
43.181, 43.183, 43.182

Silver casters, made in sets of three, were used to store and sprinkle luxurious commodities, such as sugar, pepper, and mustard. The largest caster held sugar which was sifted through the pierced dome at the top. One of the two smaller casters has a thin metal sleeve insert behind the pierced dome to prevent the scattering of the commodity within. This 'half-blind' caster would have contained dry mustard, which at the time was not sprinkled on food. Instead the cover was removed, the dry mustard spooned out, and added to vinegar to make a paste.

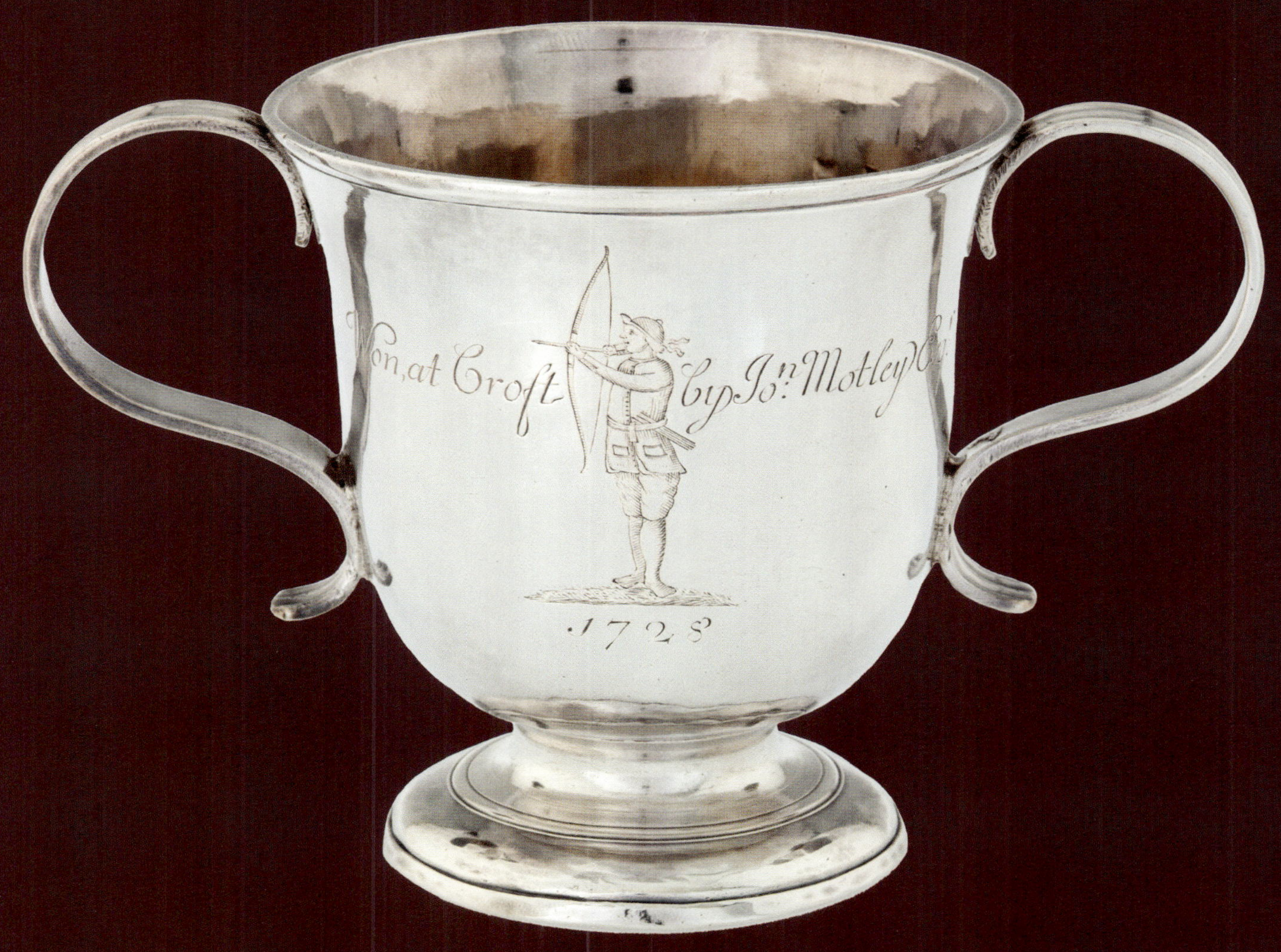

Two-handled cup, 1728–29
Made by Humphrey Payne, London, England
Silver
9.9 cm x 15.1 cm x 9.2 cm
43.96

This two-handled cup is engraved with an archer, aiming a long bow, with quiver of arrows at his waist, and inscribed 'Won at Croft by Jon. Motley, Esq., 1728'. The cup was probably awarded to 'Jon' Motely' for competing in the Antient Scorton Silver Arrow annual archery tournament in Croft-on-Tees, North Yorkshire on 5 July 1728. During the eighteenth century, aristocrats and landed gentry formed archery societies within their local counties, taking part in long-bow archery tournaments. Sixteen archers took part in the 1728 tournament, contributing a subscription fee for the running of the event and each receiving a silver cup for competing.

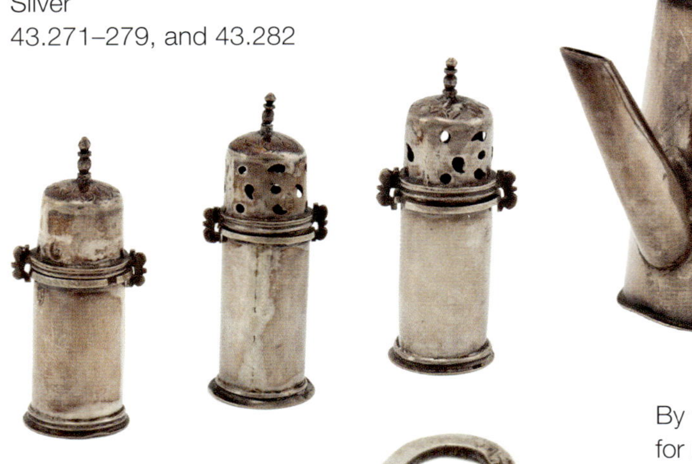

Miniature casters, snuffers and tray, monteith bowl, coffee pot, tankard and candlesticks, 1701–08

Made by George Manjoy, London, England
Silver
43.271–279, and 43.282

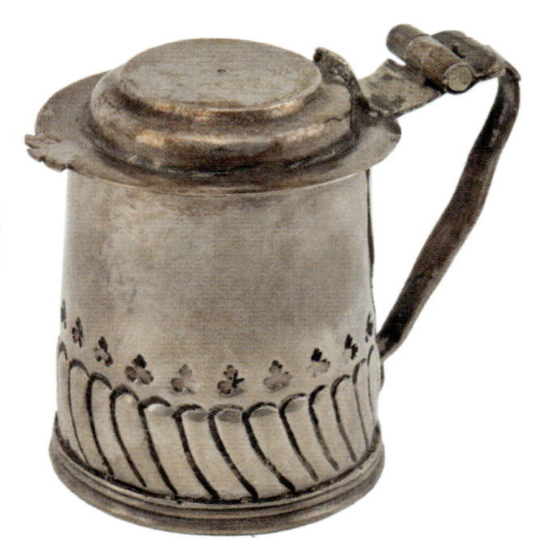

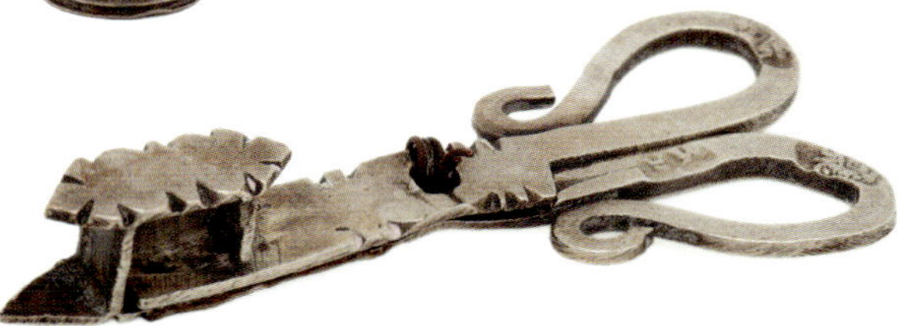

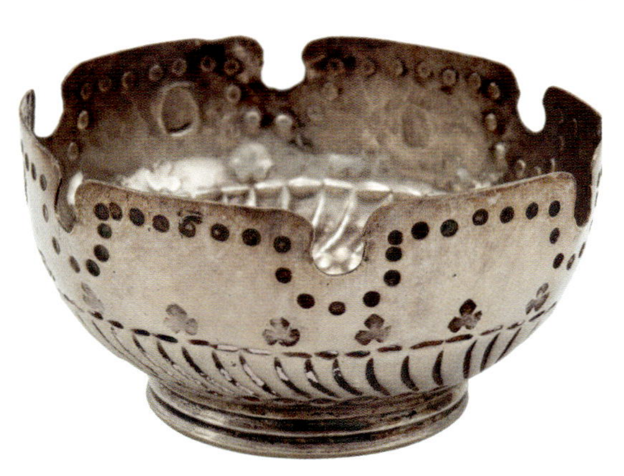

By the late-seventeenth century, there was a fashion for making silver miniatures imitating stylish tableware and utensils, crafted in the same proportions as their full-size counterparts but at tiny scale. Made as toys for dolls' houses, they were popular collectors' items for both children and adults. The Burrell Collection miniatures, purchased as a set in 1932 from dealer D.T. Sainsbury, include casters, coffee pot, candlesticks, snuffers with tray, bowl, porringer, and tankard, with the tallest miniature, a teapot and stand, reaching just over 10 centimetres in height.

Silversmith apprentices were encouraged to make miniatures to practise their craft and act as small examples to advertise their work. Due to their small size, evidence of marks can be rare but marked miniatures usually identify production by silversmiths specializing in creating miniatures. All the Burrell miniatures are marked and feature marks by George Manjoy and David Clayton, specialist London-based miniature makers during the late-seventeenth to early-eighteenth centuries. Although the miniatures from this set bear different date letter marks, it is likely they were originally collected by one person. The inscription 'P.M' is found on many of the miniatures, probably the initials of their previous owner who kept them as a set.

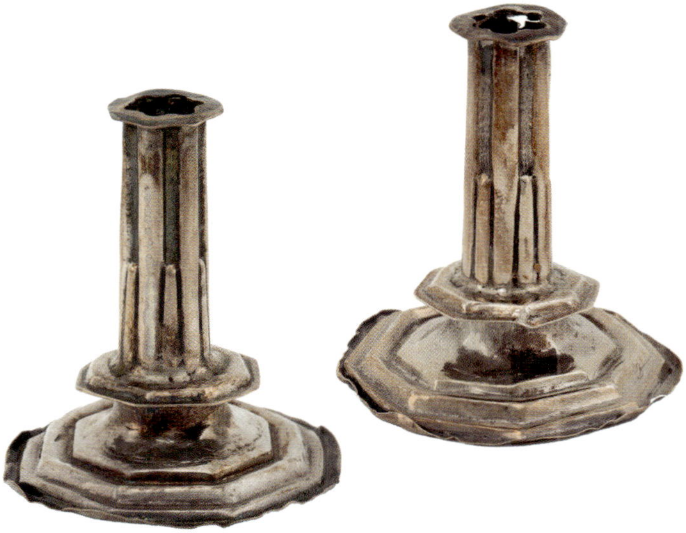

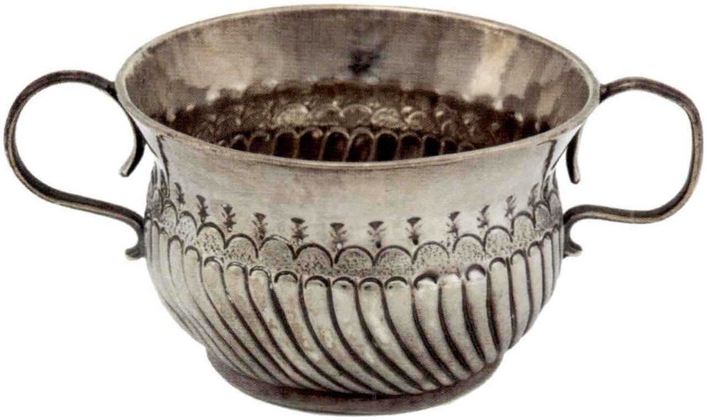

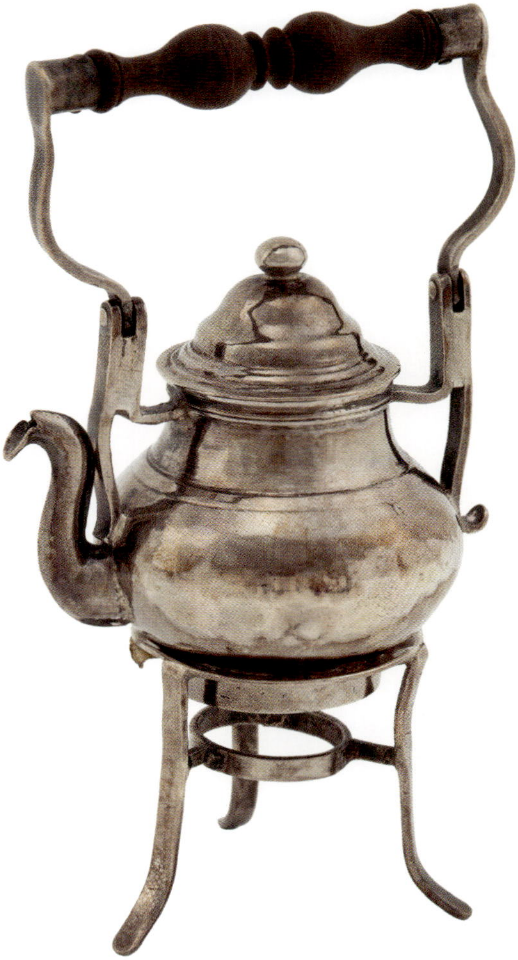

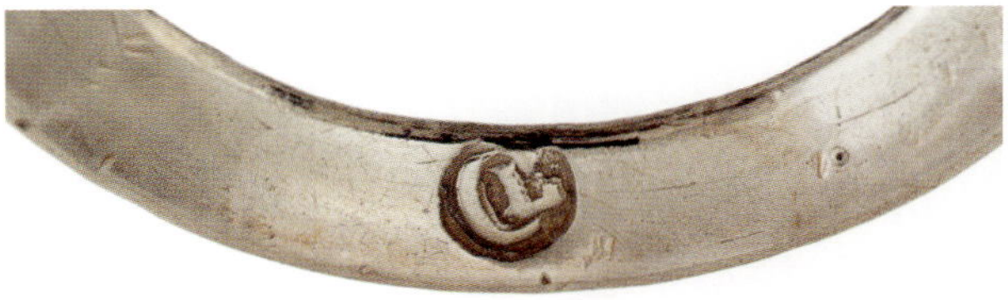

Miniature porringer, 1714–15
Made by James Goodwin, London, England
Silver
3.5 cm x 7.6 cm x 5.3 cm
43.280

Miniature teapot with stand, about 1709
Made by David Clayton, London, England
Silver
10.9 cm x 5.4 cm x 3 cm
43.281

Mark 'MA' for George Manjoy, stamped under the rim of the
miniature coffee pot.

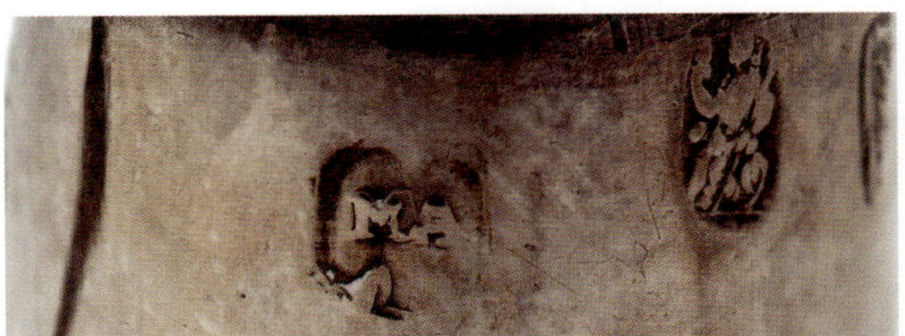

Mark 'CL' for David Clayton, stamped on the rim of the miniature
teapot stand.

Object in Focus

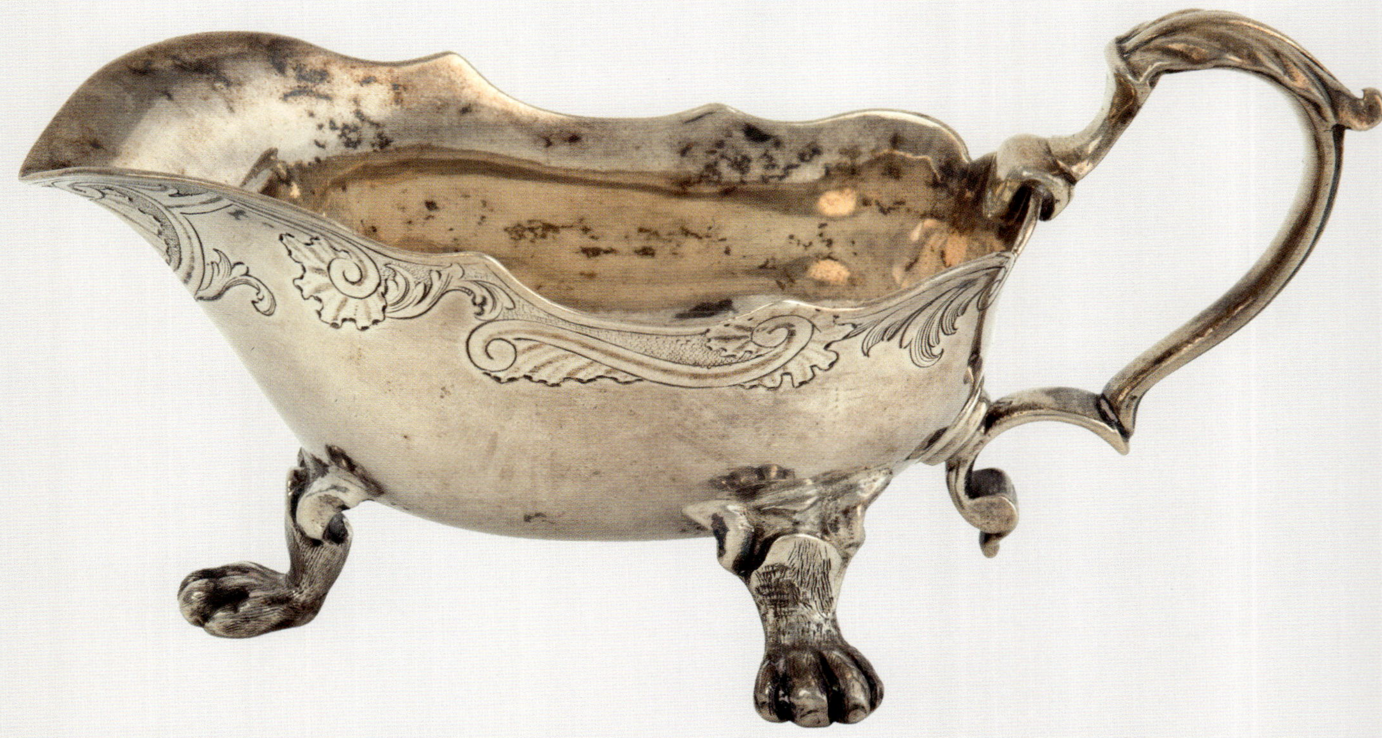

Sauceboat, 1736–37
Made by John Tuite, London, England
Silver
6.2 cm x 13.1 cm x 6 cm
43.131

The English adoption of fashionable French dining styles in the eighteenth century also influenced a change in the variety of food on offer, including rich sauces and gravy to add flavour. Sauceboats, styled after French late-seventeenth century designs, became common dining tableware, allowing the diner to serve and pour sauces as part of the meal.

This sauceboat comprises of a flattened helmet shape, so called as the body mimics the lines of an upside-down helmet of classical antiquity. Elements of rococo style, popular in the early eighteenth century, can be seen in this sauceboat. Rococo designs often included winding patterns and serpentine lines, features which make this a typical example.

It features a curved spout, scrolling brim and handle. Rococo style also drew inspiration from natural and animal forms, to create whimsical shapes and decoration. The rim is engraved with scrolling foliage and shell designs, while the bowl is supported by three 'lion feet'– the end supports shaped like lion paws. This style of three supporting feet for sauceboats became popular in the mid-eighteenth century.

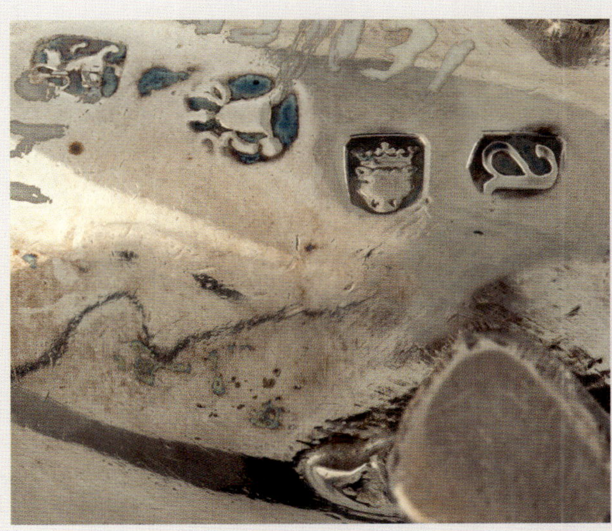

The underside of the sauceboat is marked with leopard's head crowned; lion passant; London date letter for 1736–37, and the maker's mark: a stem cup between 'JT', for London silversmith, John Tuite.

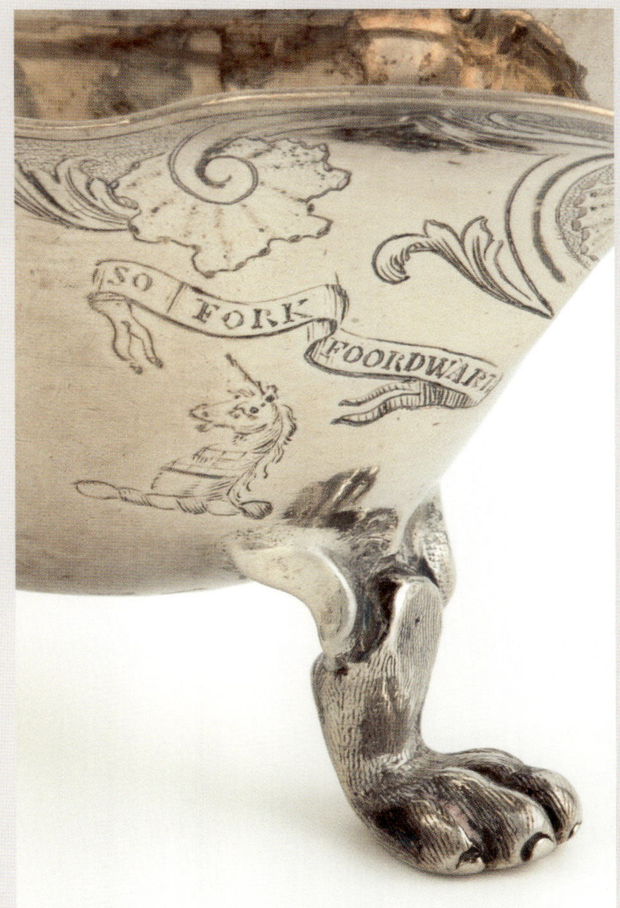

The sauceboat is engraved with a heraldic crest (unicorn's head couped argent, gorged with a collar chequy azure, and or), and motto 'SO FORK FOORDWARD', denoting possible ownership by the Cunninghame family (Scotland).

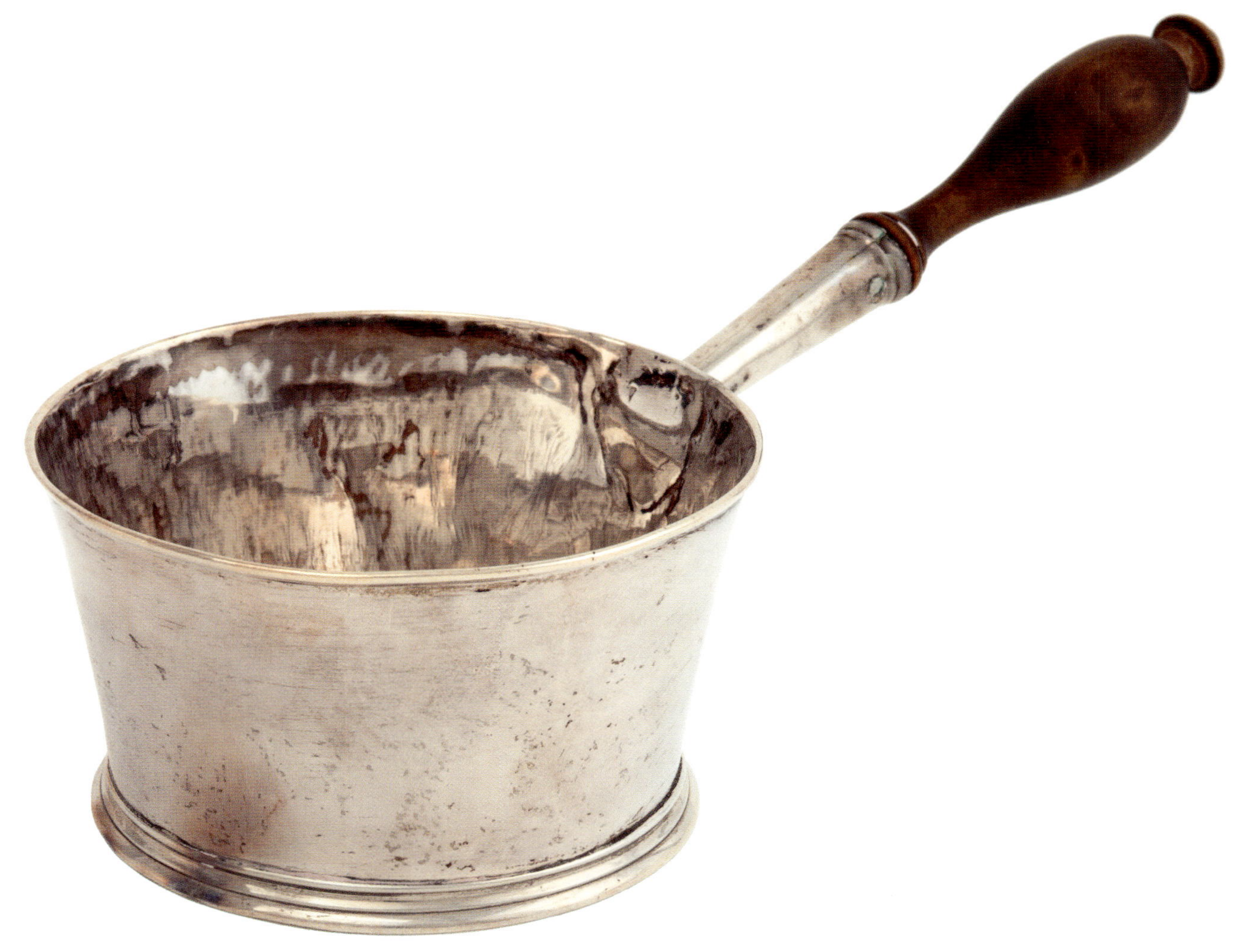

Brandy saucepan, 1725–26
Made by James Goodwin, London, England
Silver
8.2 cm x 20.7 cm x 9.5 cm
43.266

This early-eighteenth century silver saucepan of circular form has a flat bottom, slightly expanding sides, moulded foot, and everted lip. Saucepans of this type were used for warming alcohol, including wine and brandy, the heat releasing the aromatic fragrances of the liquor. In the eighteenth century, pans like this had a dual use to heat sauces and melt butters used to flavour food at meals.

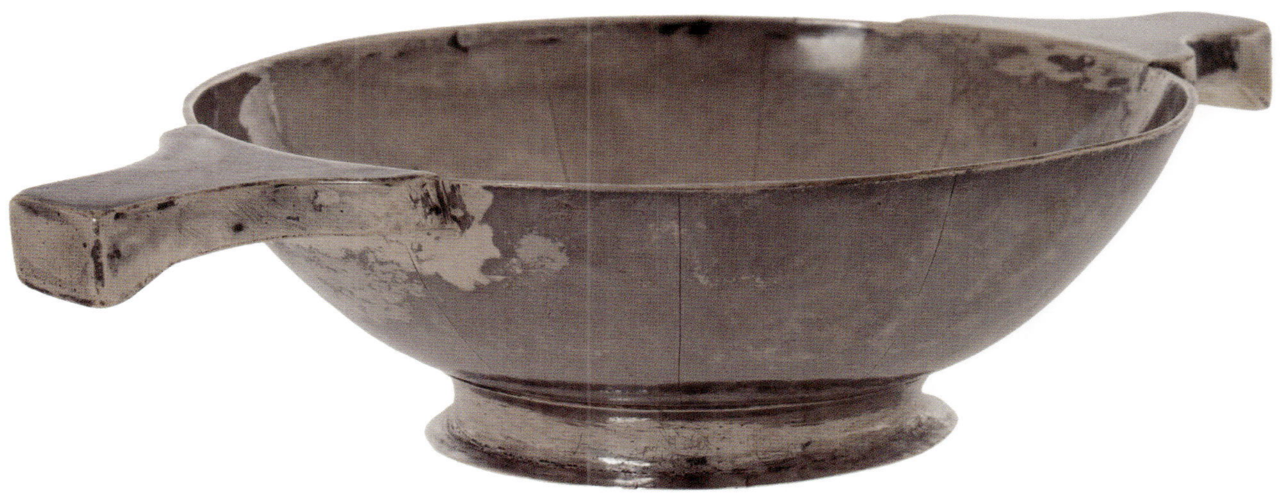

Quaich, about 1728–31

Made by William Hodgert, Glasgow, Scotland
Silver
4.6 cm x 20 cm x 12.9 cm
43.103

A quaich is a shallow drinking vessel unique to Scotland, used for ceremonial drinking, with whisky or brandy drunk from the bowl as a symbol of friendship. The name quaich stems from the Gaelic word cuach meaning cup. The quaich was passed around from person to person by the handles, known as lugs, the Scots word for ears. Quaich vessels originated traditionally in the Highlands of Scotland, often made from slotted curved wood segments, mounted in silver. This silver quaich is incised with lines to imitate the wooden segments of earlier quaiches.

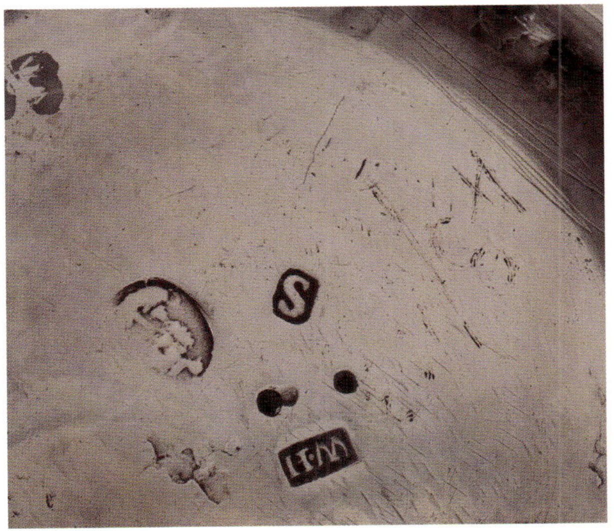

The bowl is marked with the town mark for Glasgow (the Tree, Fish and Bell), Glasgow date letter 'S', and 'W.H.', possibly for silversmith William Hodgert (or Hodgy), who was admitted to the Glasgow Incorporation of Hammermen in 1689.

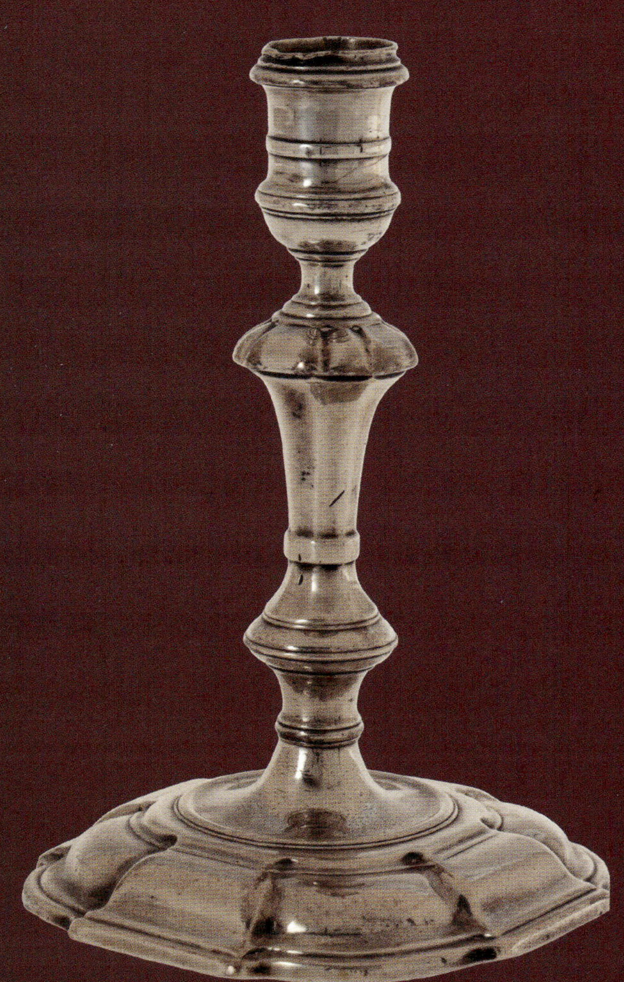

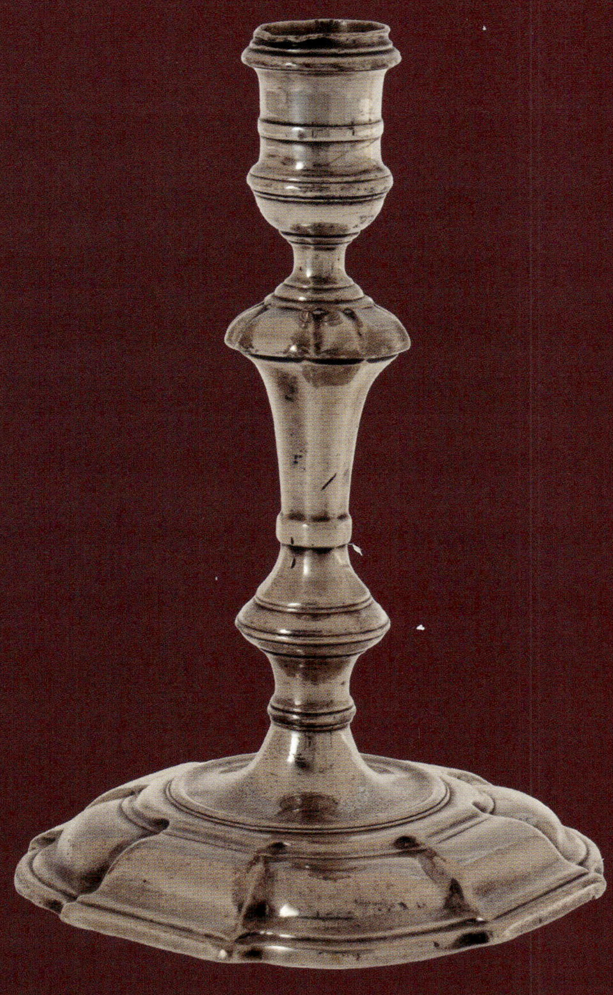

Pair of candlesticks, 1727–28
Made by James Gould, London, England
Silver
16 cm x 10.4 cm x 10.5 cm
16 cm x 10.3 cm x 10.4 cm
43.169, 43.170

Silver candlesticks were prevalent for decorating and lighting the eighteenth-century dining table, the metal further illuminating the table by reflecting the candlelight. Such candlesticks were made using casting as the main method of production, the stem with socket and foot made separately and soldered together. Casting enabled elegant forms such as the knop and baluster stem demonstrated on these candlesticks. This pair bear the mark 'IG' in monogram, for London silversmith James Gould, active from 1722–47. Gould was registered at the Goldsmiths' Hall as a 'Candlestick maker', his workshop known for specializing in candlesticks and snuffers.

Pair of tapersticks, 1712–13
Made by Thomas Merry I, London, England
Silver
11.7 cm x 7.2 cm x 7.2 cm
11.7 cm x 7 cm x 7 cm
43.175, 43.176

This pair of tapersticks have an octagonal socket on top of a stem with two knops and a facetted foot. Tapersticks are smaller formed candlesticks used to hold wax tapers, thin sticks of wax with a central wick. In the eighteenth century, tapersticks were often used for the lighting of other candles around the house or for the melting of wax required for sealing letters.

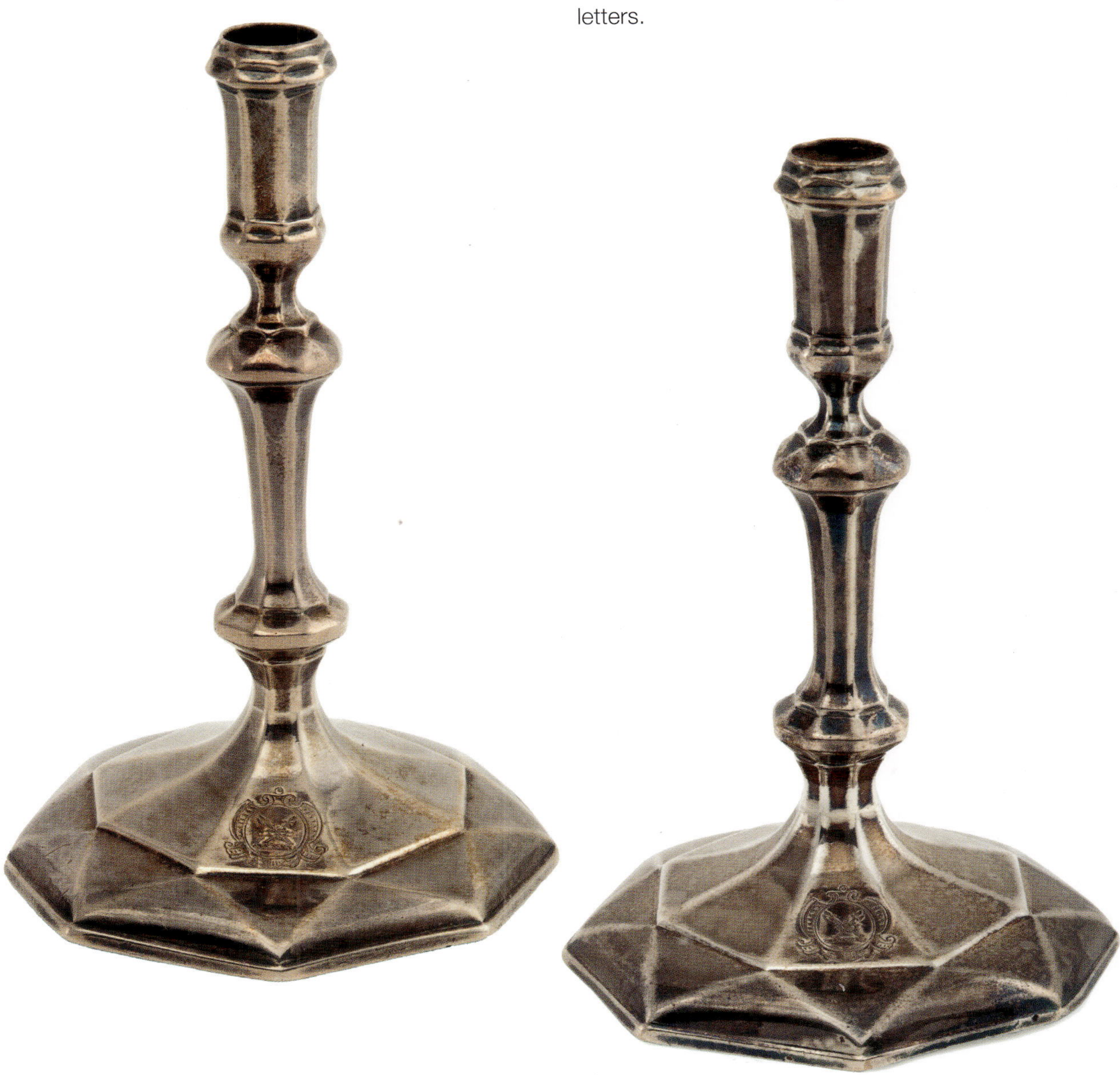

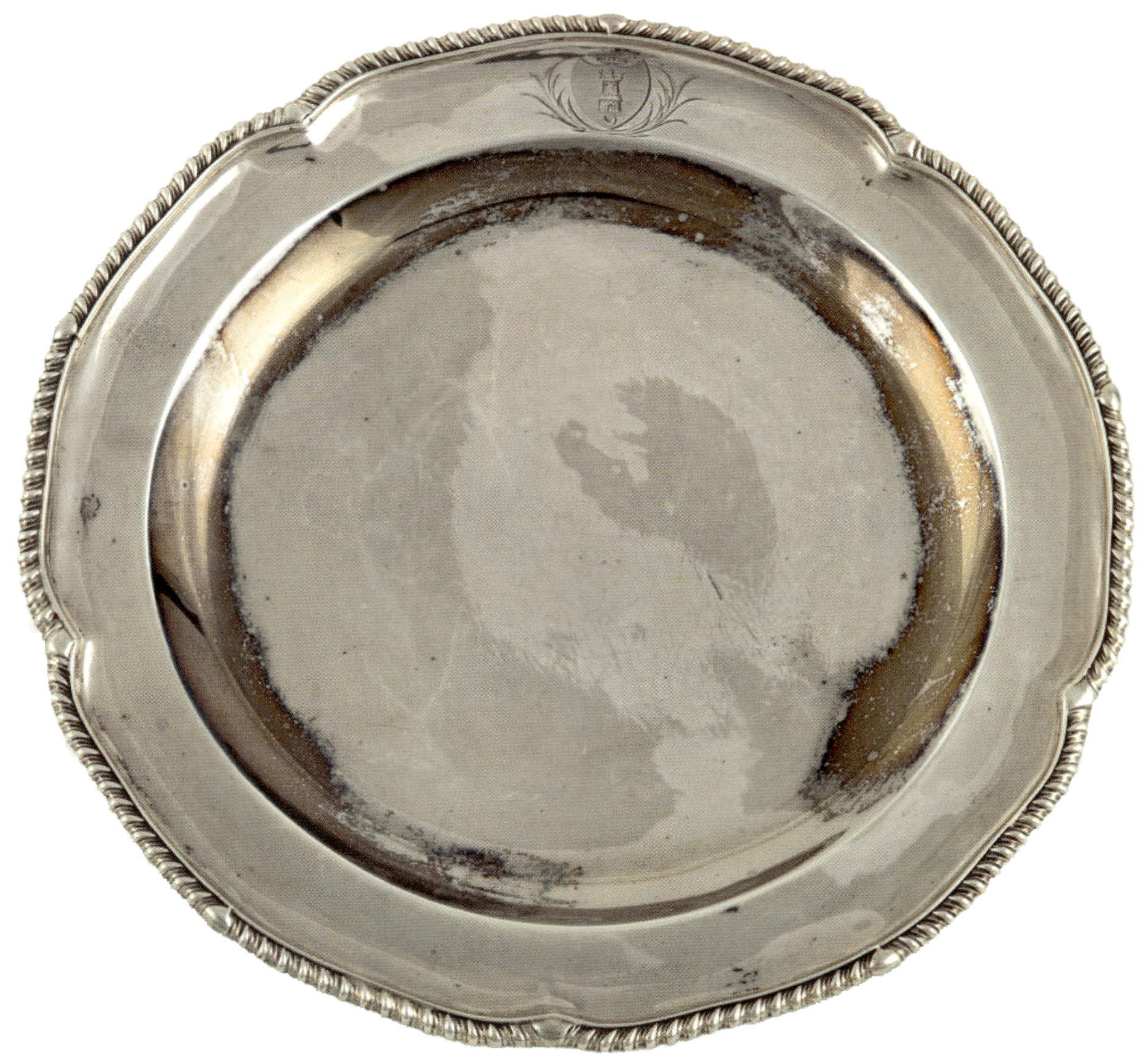

Plate with applied border, 1784–85
Made by James Young
London, England
Silver
1.3 cm x 25 cm x 25 cm
43.84

In the 1700s, porcelain or glass dining plates would often be placed upon larger silver plates. The well is sunken to hold the porcelain dish in place. As the bottom of the silver plate was covered by another dish, it was common for the well to be plain, and decoration added to the raised rim. This plate, one of a set of four, follows this design: plain except for a shaped and gadrooned fillet round edge. The high rim allowed the silver plate to be easily picked up and removed from the table by servants.

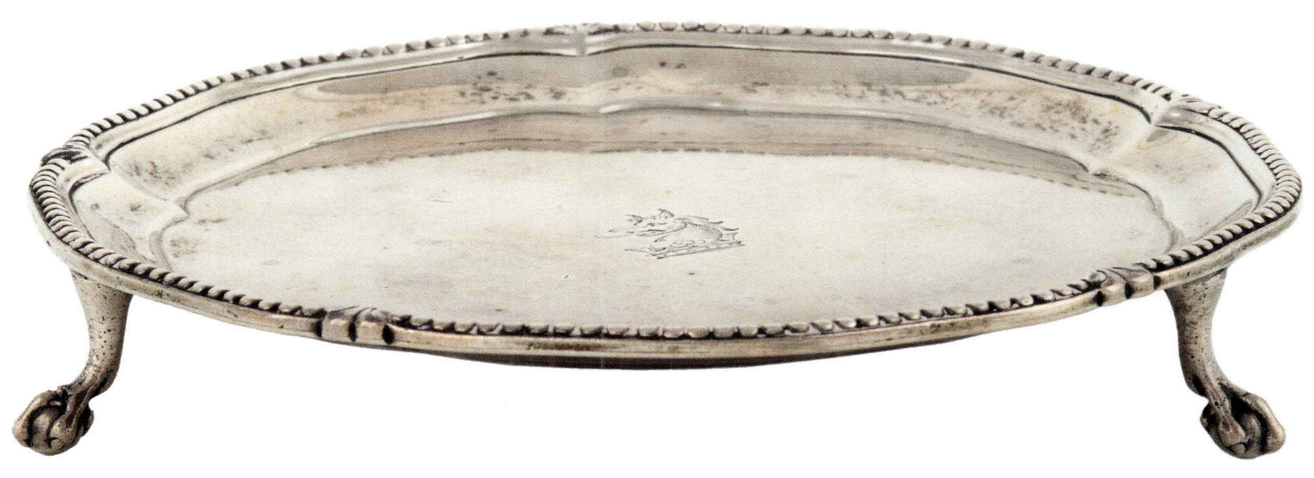

Salver, 1775–76
Made by Matthew Boulton and James Fothergill,
Birmingham, England
Silver
2.7 cm x 15.2 cm x 15.2 cm
43.76

Salvers were used as presentation dishes by servants to serve food and drinks, or present letters and cards. This salver, supported by three claw and ball feet, bears an anchor town mark for Birmingham, and the conjoined makers' mark 'MB IF' for Matthew Boulton and James Fothergill. In the 1760s, Boulton, in partnership with James Fothergill, established an extensive metalworking factory in Soho, outside of Birmingham, where he invested in modern technologies like steam engines, and organized his workers in assembly line production to mass manufacture silverware. In 1771, Matthew Boulton successfully petitioned the government to establish an assay office in Birmingham.

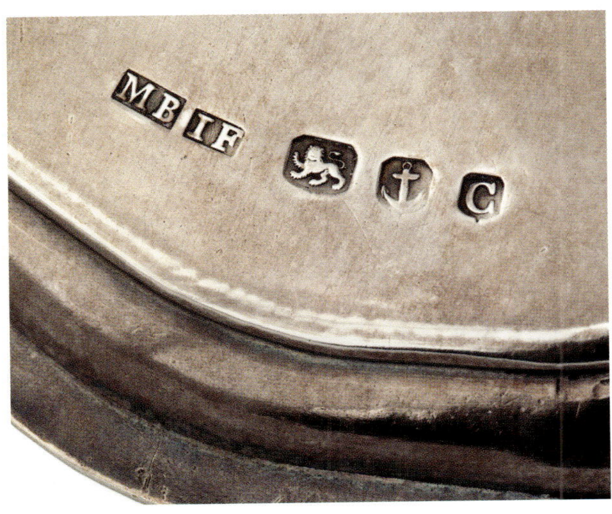

Marks on salver including anchor town mark for Birmingham.

Objects in Focus

Teapot, 1782–83
Made by William Plummer, London, England
Silver
13.2 cm x 25 cm x 9.1 cm
43.129.1

Tray, 1805–06
Made in London, England
Silver
1.7 cm x 15.3 cm x 11.4 cm
43.129.2

The thin gauge silver used to form this teapot was probably created with sheet silver from a rolling mill. From the mid-eighteenth century, the production of sheets of silver with a rolling mill helped to meet the rapidly rising demand for silver tableware. Rolling mills flattened silver ingots between two turning cylinders, pressing out thin sheets of the same thickness. The use of steam-powered rolling mills ramped up the speed of production; the silversmith was able to start with a ready-made silver sheet instead of hammering the silver flat before raising their object.

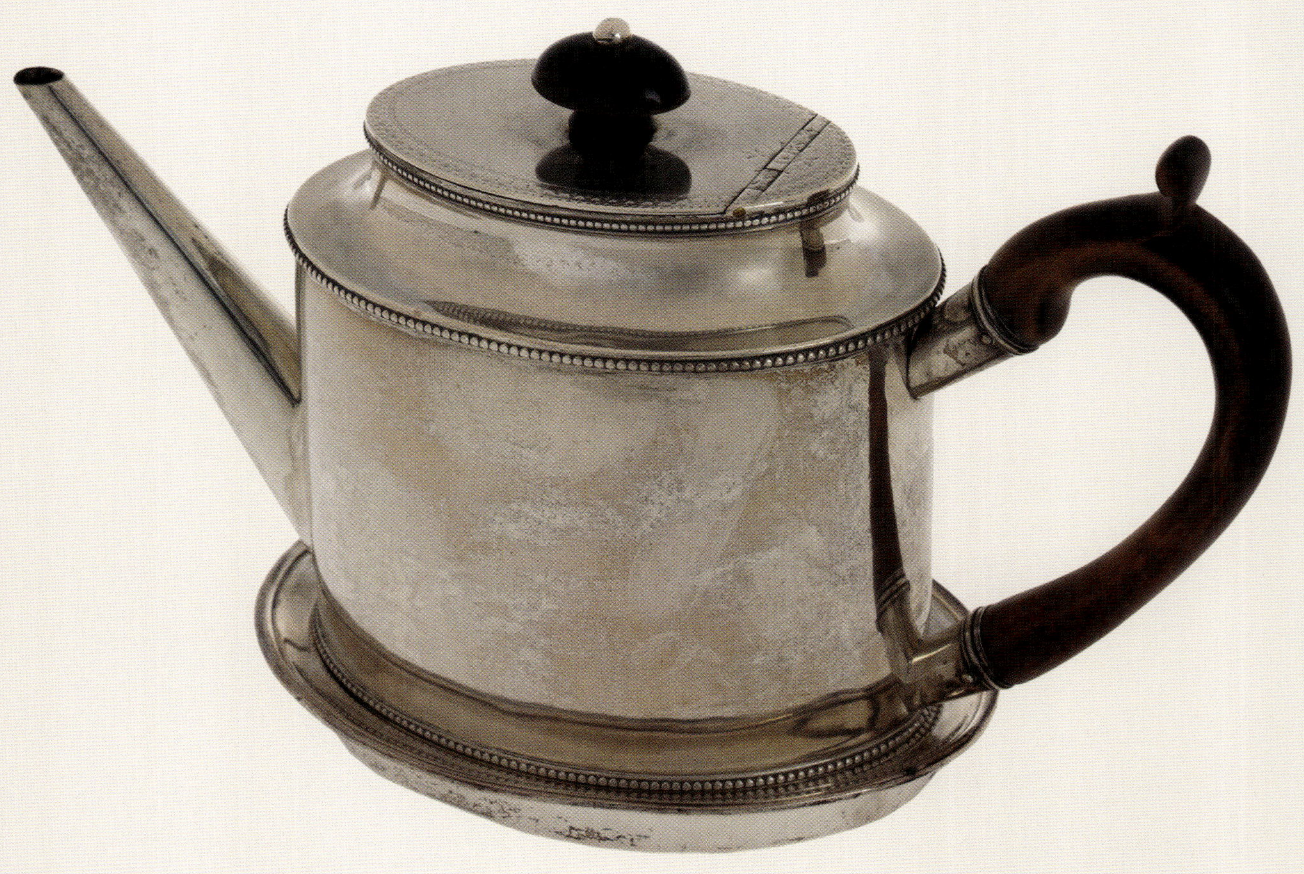

Straight-sided, thin-walled, oval-shaped tea pots, made possible by the uniformed sheet silver of rolling mills, were fashionable at the end of the eighteenth century. Most examples were designed with flat bottoms which when hot could scorch wooden tables. This teapot was sat on a silver tray to protect the surface underneath. As the fashion for taking milk with tea grew in popularity during the eighteenth century, jugs for the pouring of milk or cream became tea service essentials. This jug and teapot were some of the silver items kept by the Burrells until after their deaths, most likely used for serving their own tea.

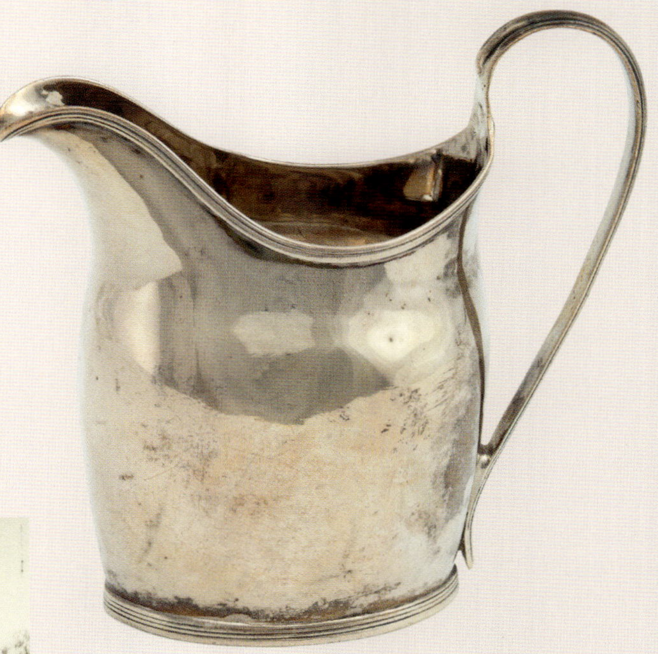

Jug, 1798–99
Made by Crispin Fuller, London, England
Silver
12.3 cm x 12.8 cm x 6.9 cm
43.114

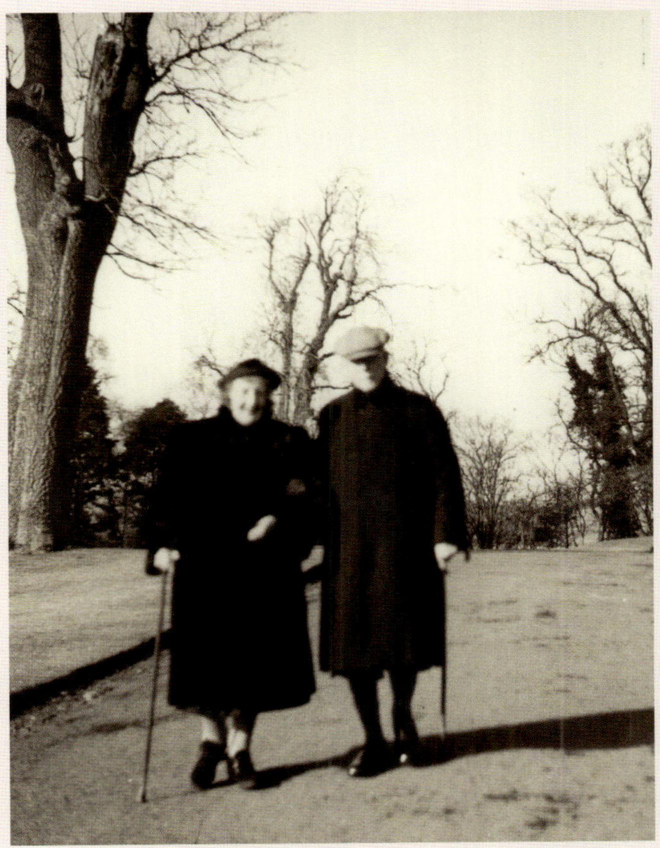

Sir William Burrell and Constance, Lady Burrell walking in the gardens of Hutton Castle, their home, about 1955.

Further Reading

Martin Bellamy and Isobel MacDonald, *William Burrell: A Collector's Life*, Glasgow Museums and Birlinn, Edinburgh, 2022. Biography of William Burrell, his life, collection and legacy.

Charles Jackson, *Silver & Gold Marks of England, Scotland & Ireland,* edited by Ian Pickford, Antique Collectors Club, 1989. A comprehensive guide to British silver hallmarks, first published in 1905, and revised in 1921, using records from national assay offices.

Pocket Edition: *Jackson's Hallmarks: English, Scottish, Irish Silver & Gold Marks from 1300 to the present day*, 2nd edition, ed. Ian Pickford, 2018. A condensed, quick reference pocket guide of Charles Jackson's work on identifying British silver hallmarks, listing cycles of marks from British assay offices.

George Dalgleish and Henry Stuart Fothringham, *Silver: Made in Scotland*, NMSE-Publishing, 2008. An exhibition catalogue from the National Museums Scotland's 2008 exhibition *Silver: Made in Scotland, exploring 500 years of Scottish silver.*

Philippa Glanville, *Silver*, V&A Publications, 2003. An accessible guide to the history of silver in Europe.

Philippa Glanville, *Silver in Tudor and Early Stuart England*, V&A Publications, 1997. An academic illustrated catalogue of the extensive Tudor and Stuart silver held in the collections of the V&A London.

Arthur G. Grimwade, *London Goldsmiths 1697–1837: Their Marks and Lives from the original registers at Goldsmiths' Hall and other sources*, Second Edition, Faber & Faber, 1982. A comprehensive record of London goldsmiths from 1697–1837, including biographies.

Christopher Hartop, *The Huguenot Legacy: English Silver 1680–1760 from the Alan and Simone Hartman Collection*, Thomas Heneage London, 1996. A catalogue of Huguenot silver from the Alan and Simone Hartman Collection, with essays exploring the social history of Huguenot silversmiths in England.